I'm Listening

How Teacher-Student Relationships Improve Reading, Writing, Speaking, and Listening

BETH PANDOLPHO

Solution Tree | Press

Copyright © 2020 by Solution Tree Press
Materials appearing here are copyrighted. With one exception, all rights are reserved. Readers may reproduce only those pages marked "Reproducible." Otherwise, no part of this book may be reproduced or transmitted in any form or by any means (electronic, photocopying, recording, or otherwise) without prior written permission of the publisher.
555 North Morton Street
Bloomington, IN 47404
800.733.6786 (toll free) / 812.336.7700
FAX: 812.336.7790
email: info@SolutionTree.com
SolutionTree.com
Visit **go.SolutionTree.com/literacy** to download the free reproducibles in this book.
Printed in the United States of America

Library of Congress Cataloging-in-Publication Data

Names: Pandolpho, Beth, author.
Title: I'm listening : how teacher-student relationships improve reading, writing, speaking, and listening / Beth Pandolpho.
Description: Bloomington, IN : Solution Tree Press, 2020. | Includes bibliographical references and index.
Identifiers: LCCN 2019043221 (print) | LCCN 2019043222 (ebook) | ISBN 9781949539394 (paperback) | ISBN 9781949539400 (ebook)
Subjects: LCSH: Teacher-student relationships. | Classroom environment--Psychological aspects. | Language arts. | Interpersonal communication.
Classification: LCC LB1033 .P326 2020 (print) | LCC LB1033 (ebook) | DDC 371.102/3--dc23
LC record available at https://lccn.loc.gov/2019043221
LC ebook record available at https://lccn.loc.gov/2019043222

Solution Tree
Jeffrey C. Jones, CEO
Edmund M. Ackerman, President

Solution Tree Press
President and Publisher: Douglas M. Rife
Associate Publisher: Sarah Payne-Mills
Art Director: Rian Anderson
Managing Production Editor: Kendra Slayton
Senior Production Editor: Tonya Maddox Cupp
Content Development Specialist: Amy Rubenstein
Copy Editor: Evie Madsen
Proofreader: Elisabeth Abrams
Text and Cover Designer: Rian Anderson
Editorial Assistant: Sarah Ludwig

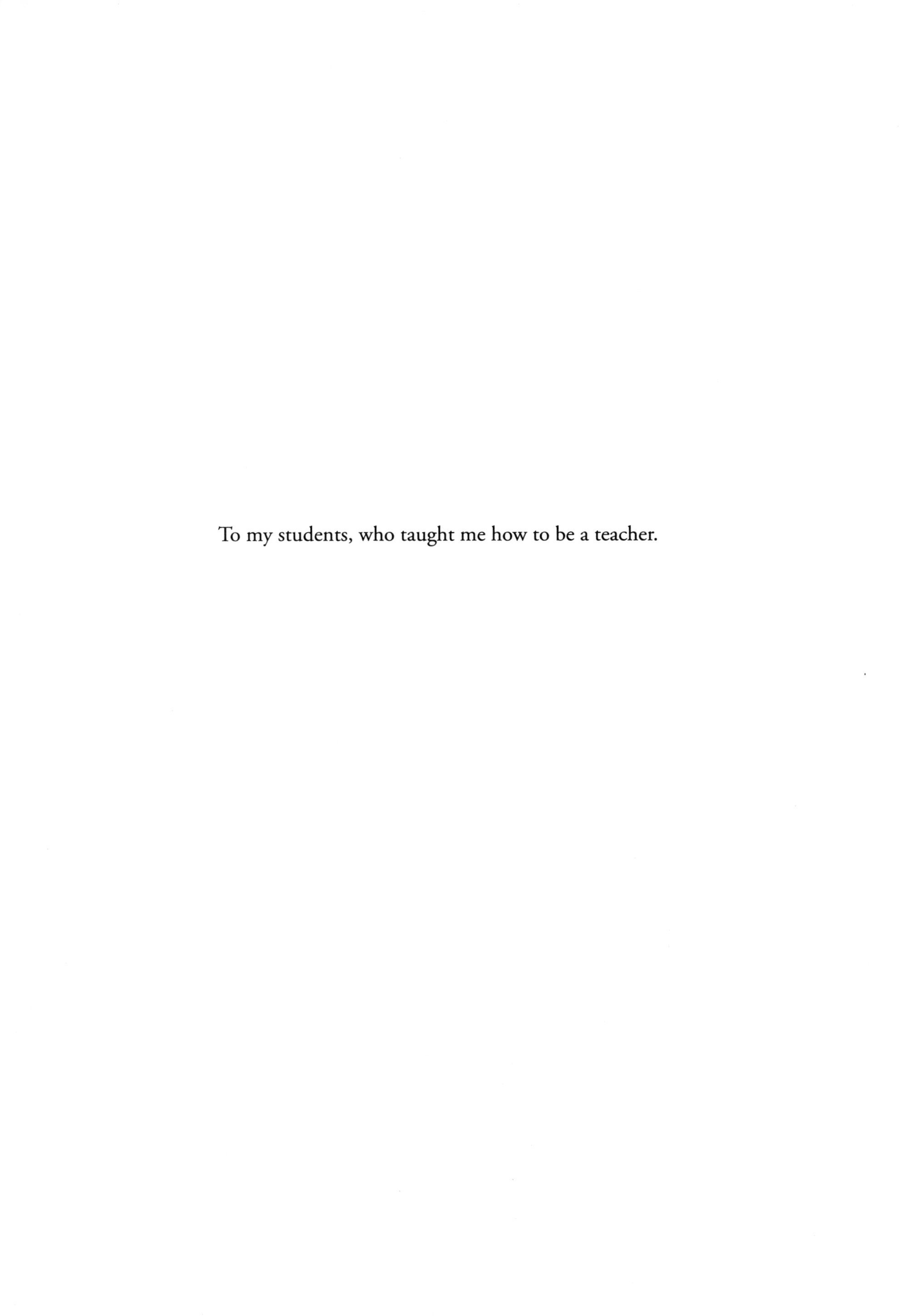

To my students, who taught me how to be a teacher.

I do think the power of teaching is in the art of listening.

—John Hattie

Acknowledgments

Thank you, Claudia Wheatley, for believing I had a book in me when I didn't believe it myself, and Amy Rubenstein, for expanding my thinking beyond what I imagined possible. To my editor, Tonya Maddox Cupp, for finding the book inside my manuscript, and to the entire staff at Solution Tree for their abundance of kindness and support. I am humbled and grateful for the opportunity to publish my first book.

Thank you to the educators who so generously shared their insights and stories: Jennifer Bard, Andrea Bean, Carl Cooper, Justin Dolcimascolo, Jonathan Ellingson, Penny Fisher, Barbara Fortunato, Marla Rae Savage Fruhling, Ellin Glassband, Kaitlyn Haley, Kate Heavers, Carolyn Hoyt, Kwame Ivery, Rebecca King, Valerie Kearns, Zachary Kumar, Kaitlin Maher, Amy Meredith, Taylor Sternotti, Stacey Tafoya, Susan Totaro, and Ashley Warren. Thank you to Micaela Blei and The Moth Teacher Institute for broadening my understanding of the power of storytelling, and for reminding me I really do know how to tell a story.

Much gratitude to my former students Sruti Bapatla, Justin Gong, Maddie Holmes, Shreyas John, Katie Lu, and Myka Melville for sharing your voices in this book to help remind us what it feels like to be a teenager.

Thank you to my children: Max, my very first editor, and to Tyler and Hope, for your patience and understanding.

To Grant Wiggins, who, through his work and enduring wisdom, challenged me to reconsider my practices and helped me truly understand how teachers can impact learning.

And to Mark Wise: so much of what's contained in these pages is what I've learned from you, and what we figured out together.

This book would not even be possible if not for the wonderfully wise and hopeful writers, thinkers, and artists who, through their work, inspire me to lend my voice to the conversation, and strive to do better as a teacher, a learner, and a citizen of the world.

Solution Tree Press would like to thank the following reviewers:

Katherine Green
English Teacher
Technical High School
St. Cloud, Minnesota

Sarah Hall
Kindergarten Teacher
Longwood Elementary School
Longwood, Florida

Jennifer Kirchoff
English Teacher
East Syracuse Minoa Central
High School
East Syracuse, New York

Kimberly Long
English Teacher
Daniel Wright Junior High School
Lincolnshire, Illinois

Trina Lovio
Instructional Services Coordinator
Panama-Buena Vista Union
School District
Bakersfield, California

Megan Menard
English Teacher
Kinard Middle School
Fort Collins, Colorado

Lori Oczkus
Author and Literacy Consultant
Reno, Nevada

Amanda Pfeiffer
English Teacher
James Bowie High School
Austin, Texas

Darby Tobolka
Instructional Coach
Akin Elementary School
Leander, Texas

Sally Wright
Educator
Pasco School District
Pasco, Washington

Visit **go.SolutionTree.com/literacy** to download the free reproducibles in this book.

Table of Contents

About the Author

Beth Pandolpho is an instructional coach at the West Windsor-Plainsboro Regional School District in New Jersey. She has taught English at the high school and college level for over twenty years. At the college level, she taught courses in remedial reading and freshman English as well as created a hybrid online course for remedial reading.

She taught a summer social justice series to high school students in her community and trained at The Moth Teacher Institute to learn how to give students a platform to speak about issues and tell their stories. Her mission is to raise students' voices by offering them authentic school experiences that mirror their real-life passions. She believes listening to students and attending to their social-emotional needs can help them thrive both personally and academically.

She has written for *Education Week*, *Educational Leadership*, and *The New York Times Learning Network*, and is a frequent contributor to Edutopia. Beth earned a bachelor's degree in English language and literature at the University of Maryland, a master's of science degree in reading at Adelphi University, and her supervisory certification for curriculum and instruction at Rutgers University.

To learn more about Beth's work, follow @bethpando on Twitter.

To book Beth Pandolpho for professional development, contact pd@SolutionTree.com.

Introduction

If you're a school teacher, and you see the beauty in those kids, they love you as a teacher, and it gets reflected, and they feel, "I'm going to do my best because this teacher sees me and gets me."

—Jack Kornfield

Our students need teachers who are good role models and listeners. Our students need teachers who are facilitators and coaches who design learning experiences that inspire and engage them in the repeated practice that causes learning. Our students need teachers who design from desired outcomes not only for learning but also for classroom culture. And I've come to believe—and research bears out—that strong relationships and a sense of belonging are among the most important tools teachers have to impact learning (Rolland, 2012). These understandings have made teaching and learning both joyful and rewarding for me . . . and I hope for my students.

Relationship building and worthwhile and ambitious academic experiences are not mutually exclusive. Instead, when you purposefully integrate both strong relationships and a sense of belonging into the classroom culture and lesson design, they can motivate students to persevere through demanding coursework.

Student engagement further increases when teachers give students choices in process and product driven by their interests and readiness levels. Research shows "control leads to compliance; autonomy leads to engagement . . . Only engagement can produce mastery" (Pink, 2009, pp. 108–109). A classroom built on the foundation of strong relationships and belonging provides a safe place for students to take intellectual and emotional risks, make mistakes, and feel supported as they forge ahead to derive meaning from content.

Students need teachers who care about them, are sensitive to their needs, and think far beyond delivering content and imparting skills. Students need teachers who intentionally create a learning environment in which students' presence and voices matter. Students need teachers who can help them better understand themselves and the world around them by providing complex and challenging learning experiences while at the same time including opportunities for ownership, personal connection, and growth. This environment is particularly important for refining literacy skills, as the repeated practice of speaking, listening, reading, and writing often requires students to be courageous and make themselves vulnerable. That work can be intensely personal.

This book demonstrates how to intentionally build strong relationships with students and create a sense of belonging in the classroom while maintaining a challenging academic environment through lesson design, classroom routines, expectations, and learning activities. Teachers will learn how to work toward creating a classroom that balances relationships, a sense of belonging, and challenging coursework, so students can work to develop the grit and resilience necessary to become engaged and thoughtful citizens, find meaning and purpose in life, and withstand and transcend the challenges ahead.

A Shift in Thinking

One of my students wrote a persuasive piece outlining the detrimental effects of stress on high school students. The primary task was to convey the seriousness of the issue and change the readers' thinking about the subject. My student's first attempt didn't make me believe his life was any more stressful than mine. When he asked me for feedback, I responded, "I get it that you're tired and stressed, but so am I. Help me understand. Make me feel what it's like to be a high school student."

We had read *The Odyssey* (Homer, 8th century BC/1999) earlier that year, and his mind was swirling with bronze-tipped spears, golden-winged sandals, and shipwrecks, because in his next draft he wrote, "Stress is a three-pronged blade of parental expectations, teacher requirements, and competitive peers." He termed stress the "tension-laded trident" and wrote, "I could feel the trident digging in my back . . . prodding me through the corridors. Weighed down by projects, tests, deadlines . . ." I cringed as I read on. He ended his piece with, "Just imagine what students could accomplish with warm, supportive hands on our backs, lifting us up instead." He innocently asked me if his edits had helped me understand. I sighed, as I said, "Yes. Yes, I understand now."

During the 2014–2015 year in my school district, which has about 9,900 students:

> 120 middle and high school students were recommended for mental health assessments; 40 were hospitalized. And on a survey administered by the district, students wrote things like, "I hate going to school," and "Coming out of 12 years in this

> district, I have learned one thing: that a grade, a percentage or even a point is to be valued over anything else." (Spencer, 2015)

These statistics are not unique to my district. According to the National Institute of Mental Health (n.d.), around 3.2 million adolescents had at least one major period of depression in 2017. And, according to the American Academy of Pediatrics (2017), "The number of children and adolescents admitted to children's hospitals for thoughts of suicide or self-harm more than doubled" since 2007. Suicide is the second leading cause of adolescent death in the world (Hawton, Saunders, & O'Connor, 2012), but in combination with other protective factors, connectedness and support can help (Centers for Disease Control and Prevention, n.d.).

As teachers, often we can barely keep our heads above our grading, planning, parental concerns, and administrative responsibilities. Yet one thing I know for sure is that I don't want to be one of the three prongs of the trident digging into my students' backs. Educational research clearly indicates attending to students' social-emotional needs is inextricably linked to learning:

> A positive, caring, respectful climate in the classroom is a prior condition to learning. Without students' sense that there is a reasonable degree of 'control,' sense of safety to learn, and sense of respect and fairness that learning is going to take place, there is little chance that much positive is going to occur. (Hattie, 2012, p. 70)

If we can try to better understand our students and their perspectives and show them, in very specific ways, that we respect and value them, we can open a pathway to learning.

It can be difficult to accept that some of our long-held beliefs and tried-and-true practices may no longer best fulfill our students' needs. Our teaching philosophy and approaches are tangled up with our identity and intertwined with our ego, and any hint that we are not already doing our job as well as we can might feel like a personal attack. However, our students are managing different demands, and this requires a change in our approach. Does this suggest we have been failing at our primary mission? Of course not. But it does mean if we listen to the research with an open mind and make some small changes, we can do even better. Over the years, I've been watching and learning from my students, trying to understand what's working in my classroom and why. I am, probably much like you, both a participant and an observer.

What Makes This Book Different

This book draws inspiration from writers, psychologists, and educators about the importance of relationships and belonging, and intertwines these philosophies and applies them to the classroom. Each chapter provides strategies and resources for immediate use, along with reflective questions at the end to help you consider how to implement these ideas in your classroom. Also, educational research supports each strategy and approach. They are linked to common state standards and modeled through my own teaching practices along with those of other teachers, which helps you visualize how you might incorporate similar moves into your practice. Each strategy and approach is supported by educational research.

This book is not about giving students stickers and trophies for just showing up or offering meaningless praise for a job not particularly well done. You don't need to be a certain kind of teacher in order to adopt these approaches. The purpose for working to create a student-centered classroom founded on strong relationships and a sense of belonging is so students will work hard and persist through the often difficult work of becoming a more proficient reader, writer, speaker, and listener. It is so students know it's OK to make mistakes, failure is part of learning, and there is no such thing as a stupid question. It is so teachers can offer feedback to students that may be hard to hear, but students will listen because they know our primary mission is to further their personal and academic growth. Feedback improves learning only if it's acted upon, and these relationships enable students to accept feedback that is critical to learning.

In This Book

This book offers ideas and approaches to grades 6–12 teachers for reading, writing, speaking, and listening—skills that apply across disciplines—to consider as they shift the way they deliver content while honoring the curriculum integrity and course expectations. This book identifies the critical components that work together to create a synergy to advance learning: build relationships and establish a sense of belonging, so students will feel secure enough to engage in the kind of deep and meaningful learning with the potential to result in transfer to their lives beyond school. We'll explore these components throughout the book, and each chapter slowly unfolds to show how relationships and belonging support literacy development.

Each chapter offers research-based activities and reproducibles for immediate use to build relationships and belonging as well as to teach reading, writing, speaking, and listening skills across the disciplines and grade levels. Each chapter also offers insights and strategies designed to inspire teachers to make small changes in their classroom to enhance students' interest level and motivation. Reflective questions at the end of each chapter help teachers consider how to implement and adapt these approaches to improve the classroom experience for students as well as for themselves. Throughout the book, student voices from across grade levels will show teachers how relationships and belonging impact their educational experiences. Similarly, K–12 teachers have shared their ideas to illustrate how teaching strategies and ideas designed to build relationships and belonging transcend grade levels and can inspire teachers to make subtle changes that make a real difference in student learning.

The book has two parts: (1) "Building the Foundation for Where Learning Begins" and (2) "Supporting the Development of Literacy Skills Built on the Foundation of Relationships and Belonging." Part I focuses on why strong relationships with students and establishing a comprehensive sense of belonging are foundational to learning. It also includes strategies and ideas that show how to seamlessly incorporate these elements into your teaching practice and lesson design. Part II's literacy strategies reflect the paradigm shift to a more student-centered classroom. To make this necessary shift, we need to first lay the groundwork for this intricate support system of relationships and belonging. In accordance with American psychologist Abraham H. Maslow's (1943) hierarchy of needs, this kind of classroom culture meets students' basic and psychological needs and empowers students to envision the possibilities of who they can become.

Part I holds chapters 1–3; part II holds chapters 4–6. The chapters break down as follows.

- Chapter 1 shares how the intersection of my teaching experience, backward design (Wiggins & McTighe, 2005), and research led me to conclude the approaches discussed in this book empower teachers to have the greatest impact on students' lives.
- Chapter 2 offers strategies for building relationships with students in a professional capacity as well as suggestions for classroom activities and routines to support relationships. This chapter will also discuss how relationships with students enable teachers to have difficult conversations and offer critical feedback to enhance student performance.
- Chapter 3 demonstrates how teachers create a sense of belonging by establishing classroom routines and designing activities to foster students' connection to the class, themselves, others, and the work. Research from Maslow (1943) to University of Houston professor Brené Brown (2010, 2017, 2018) supports each strategy and shows how a carefully designed classroom culture can fulfill students' basic human need to belong, which is a prerequisite for learning.
- Chapter 4 focuses on how reading is the great unifier—and how proficient reading across the disciplines leads to success. Included are close reading

activities for immediate use across texts. It also shows how teachers can enable students to identify and adopt the specific reading strategies they need.

- Chapter 5 examines the difficulty of teaching writing and offers methods for motivating students to invest more deeply in their writing by offering choices and writing for authentic purposes and audiences. Suggestions for making feedback more manageable and effective are here as well.
- Chapter 6 discusses why speaking and listening should get more attention from teachers, and how to encourage student voice. It offers ideas and strategies teachers can immediately use to foster speaking and listening skills.
- The epilogue reinforces the research that says a student-centered classroom built on strong relationships and belonging has the capacity to impact literacy development and positively affect student learning.
- In the appendix, read stories from teachers across grade levels and disciplines who seamlessly integrate relationships and belonging in their lesson design, and listen to their students' triumphs.

You certainly won't find all the answers here, but I do believe listening to the research, our students, and our colleagues is a good place to start. We all need supportive colleagues to offer us new ideas and insights whether we find them in the faculty room, the classroom next door, or inside the pages of a book. I hope this book offers you renewed excitement about the possibilities of our profession to impact students and learning. I also hope the strategies and stories in this book inspire you to share your insight and wisdom with me, because . . . I'm listening.

Part I

Building the Foundation for Where Learning Begins

This hour I tell things in confidence, I might not tell everybody, but I will tell you.
—Walt Whitman

Appreciating Why Relationships Matter in School

I've been a teacher since 1996, and still, I agonize over what to do on the first day of school. What should be my opening remarks? Should I distribute the supply list on the first day? Should I discuss class policies and procedures? Do I want to spend the entire first day on introductory activities and icebreakers, or does doing this give the impression that my class is not a serious one? The teacher next door likes to distribute the class novel on the very first day. She confidently reports, "There's no time to waste. Right?" I stammer in response, "Right. . . ."

But is that right?

I can't even bear to think about what to do the second day! Why, after so many years, do I still not have this entirely figured out? Maybe it's because each school year promises a new beginning. We can repair what was broken, perfect what we've done right, and try something we've always wanted to try. But there is so much to consider, the success rate is questionable, and it is all so overwhelming. And no matter how much I plan, I am immobilized as I marvel at the enormous responsibility of educating other people's children.

Ever since I was a new teacher, abiding by guiding principles and philosophies has helped ground me. Then, when I would falter or doubt myself, I could rely on these guidelines to serve as bumpers—like the ones for children in the bowling alley or the flippers in a pinball machine that keep the ball in play—keeping me in the game. This chapter illustrates what I learned through trial and error, the lessons that ultimately culminated into the philosophy that is the underpinning of this book—relationships matter.

Understanding by Design

I used to only think about the final assessment as I approached the end of a unit. When I happened across the Understanding by Design (UbD) framework by award-winning coauthors Grant Wiggins and Jay McTighe (2005), it completely shifted my thinking. According to McTighe (2015), "The idea is to plan backward from worthy goals—transferable concepts, principles, processes, and essential questions that will enable students to apply their learning in meaningful and authentic ways." Surprisingly, planning backward can be enormously calming because you always know exactly what your students need to know and do to be successful.

I realized that if I decide the final assessment at the beginning of the unit, I can design opportunities over the course of the unit to prepare students for the end I have in mind. At the end of a language arts unit, if students need to memorize and recite a Shakespearean monologue, then during the unit, students should practice analyzing the rhythm of Shakespeare's language, determining how it lends itself to memorization, and perform short scenes. At the end of a unit in science, if students need to complete a science lab independently, then throughout the unit I should model and offer students time to practice each component, so they are fully prepared for the final performance task. For me, designing with the end in mind offers a distinct focus and infuses purpose into each of my lesson-planning decisions.

This strategy had the additional benefit of helping me confidently address my students' questions. I actually knew the answers when they asked, "Will we have to know this for the test?", "Are we going to have to memorize and recite an entire monologue?" or "Will we be able to work together?" Over time, my commitment to designing with the end in mind showed my students that they could trust me, and this continued reassurance strengthened our relationships. The UbD framework helped my students recognize that I was a competent teacher who was true to my word and whose primary goal was to set them up for success.

This year I'm learning the most because I think my teacher knows what it feels like to be a kid. —Fifth grader

Over time, I noticed I was intuitively applying this philosophy to every decision in my classroom. With planning with the end in mind as my guiding philosophy, when I began to feel overwhelmed by minutiae or questioned my judgment, I asked myself these questions.

- "Why did I set this policy or expectation in my class?"
- "What's the purpose of this desk arrangement or that technology tool?"
- "Is this decision in the service of meeting my larger goals?"

And by asking myself these questions, I design each lesson, activity, procedure, and even the posters in my room to reach the end I have in mind.

How It's About You . . . But It Isn't

If I had met Wiggins (2013) when I was a new teacher and he told me, "the teacher is merely one resource for learning, no different from a book, a peer, an experience, or an experimental result," I would have thought—with more than a modicum of certainty—he had no idea what he was talking about. If my twenty-something-year-old-self had the nerve to raise her hand and say, "You can't really mean the teacher is no more important than a book" and he firmly held his position, I would have held back the tears and asked myself if this teacher development was some kind of perverse hazing ritual.

I imagine he might add, to further my discomfort, "No matter what the teacher says or does, the learner has to engage with and process the 'teaching' if learning is to happen" (Wiggins, 2013).

What?

Wiggins (2013) continues, "The teaching is a stimulus. . . . It is the learner who decides to try to learn (or not) from what happens," admitting this is "unromantic," but maintaining "the learning is the center of our world, not the teaching."

It's not the teaching?

But, I write the plans, design the activities, and create the assignments. I encourage and uplift! I reassure and console! I do the work to make sure the lesson is interesting and not boring—inspiring and not draining. I even tell jokes sometimes! How am I not the center of this experience? Clearly, Wiggins (2013) doesn't realize I became a teacher to be Michelle Pfeiffer in *Dangerous Minds* (Simpson, Bruckheimer, & Smith, 1995) and to call out to my despondent students, "There are no victims in this classroom!"

But it's still a little about me. Right?

As it turns out . . . yes, it is. Yet, perhaps not as the protagonist of some teacher narrative as I originally thought.

What I've come to realize is that Wiggins (2013) is right; teachers are a part of the lesson design; however, if we reflect on John Hattie's (2012) assertion, "a positive respectful environment is a prior condition to learning" (p. 70), it follows that teachers are the only part of this design with the ability to create a positive classroom environment. Hence, teachers are the part of the design that makes all of the other pieces—the books, experiences, and experiments—work. Teachers are the heart of the design that pumps life into the other parts, and the other parts don't even exist without the teacher.

(Although sometimes I still wish I were Michelle Pfeiffer.)

I really don't have a specific teacher that made a difference in my life. All my teachers helped me throughout the years. If they didn't, I wouldn't be where I am today. —Twelfth grader

---

In the spirit of designing with the end in mind, I began asking myself more questions.

- "What do I want students to know and do by the end of the year?"
- "How do I create experiences so students feel connected to the content, and so all students actively engage to construct meaning for themselves?"
- "How do I want students to feel about themselves and the work we're doing together in my class?"

And then I ask myself the bigger question.

- "How do all the design elements (including me) work together to engage students in deepening their understanding, and ultimately transferring this knowledge to their lives beyond school?"

It seemed to me if everything about the learning experience is a part of the design, then we need to assemble the pieces correctly. I sought to identify the essential components of the learning experience I want for my students, and then try to place them in order, but not in order of importance, but instead what needs to exist for the other elements to work—for example, like the inner workings of a clock in which each of the parts are interconnected and depend on each other to function effectively. With the notion of this complex set of gears as my guiding metaphor, I work to identify each of the pieces and how they work together to keep me in the game and to reach the end I have in mind.

I now begin every school year by establishing relationships and belonging.

Teachers, Relationships, and Learning

Teacher-student relationships are foundational to learning. When teachers know and understand their students, they can determine entry points for engagement. When students know and understand their teachers, they are affected by their teacher's dedication to learning and accept critical feedback because they recognize it is designed to help them improve. Barbara L. McCombs (1995) states that "almost everything [teachers] do in the classroom has a motivational influence on students—either positive or negative" (p. 5).

When I think of my own school days, I don't at all remember how to solve a quadratic equation, the difference between mass, density, and volume, or how to conjugate the verb être. But I do remember the teachers who taught me. According to researchers Linda Darling-Hammond and Channa M. Cook-Harvey (2018), student-teacher relationships:

> Help develop the emotional, social, behavioral, and cognitive competencies foundational to learning. In addition, students need a sense of physical and psychological safety for learning to occur because fear and anxiety undermine cognitive capacity and short-circuit the learning process. Students learn best when they can connect what happens in school to their cultural contexts and experiences, when their teachers are responsive to their strengths and needs, and when their environment is "identity safe," reinforcing their value and belonging. (p. 15)

I remember in high school when Mr. Salerno, my social studies teacher, told us segregation still exists. We didn't believe him, so he began listing the demographics of towns in our area. When he asked us to look around the cafeteria and notice who was sitting with whom, I noticed the sea of white students and the two tables of brown students who sat together in the back. I never looked at the world the same way again.

And I'll never forget Mr. McAuliffe, my twelfth-grade creative writing teacher, who after reading my work told me I should be a writer. At seventeen, my vision of my own writing didn't extend beyond my composition notebook and the journal I kept in my nightstand. But I never forgot his words or his confidence in me. It's still easier to channel his confidence in my ability than my own confidence. It was his class and his teaching that inspired me to become a teacher. I still do things with my students I learned from him. I'd like to think Mr. McAuliffe would be proud of me for being a writer and a teacher.

My science teacher makes us think. If you ask her a question, she will give a counter-question and that will make you think and find out the answer for yourself, which helps you understand better. —Seventh grader

---

The best teachers challenge students and broaden their perspective. The teachers we all love and admire help us see ourselves and the world in ways we haven't imagined because we trust them—sometimes more than we trust ourselves.

And how does learning impact teachers?

The vulnerability required for students to learn is equally true for teachers. As teachers, we must be open to being wrong and understand that being wrong is not an assault on our character, but an awakening toward more effective learning. What we believe about education and how to best teach is firmly ingrained. And if we learn what we believe is wrong, the consequences of doing our job wrong or not as effectively as we could might be painful. This is because it is not only a criticism of who we are but also because of the implication that we have been negatively affecting students' lives—or at the very least not doing our job as effectively as we could. National Teacher of the Year in 2015 Shanna Peeples (as cited in Ferlazzo, 2018) says, "Learning—true learning—carries risk and requires vulnerability. . . . The answers we seek are often inside ourselves, our colleagues, and our students."

Teaching is so much more than delivering content or imparting skills. Reciprocity between teachers and students, a shared experience, maximizes learning. I bring my imperfect self to class every day so my students can show up imperfect as well. I love going to work because every day I learn something new or see things from a perspective I hadn't before considered.

In my classroom, my students and I talk about "daring greatly" (Roosevelt, 1910, p. 57) and *failing forward*, or failing well (Maxwell, 2007). We talk about how successful people try things unsuccessful people do not. We talk about how not being chosen for the soccer team often has more to do with the coach's assessment of our size and agility instead of being a statement of our worth as human beings. We all do average work—sometimes on tests, sometimes on essays, and sometimes in our daily interactions. However, these external performance indicators do not define us. They are a snapshot of one moment in time. I assure students even if they get a C on a paper, I still think they are A+ people. And if they think back to some of my lessons, even though I tried, they might very well give me a C.

We all have our moments; there are always other moments.

Relationships and Feedback

Strong relationships allow teachers to give students honest feedback and tell them things that are sometimes difficult to hear. This is often exactly the feedback students need to help them progress. Researcher and author Carol S. Dweck (2015) advises:

> Too often nowadays, praise is given to students who are putting forth effort, but *not learning*, in order to make them feel

good in the moment: "Great effort! You tried your best!" It's good that the students tried, but it's not good that they're not learning.

I had a student who was despondent because she had received a B instead of an A. I struggled to move her focus beyond the grade, and asked if she was ready to hear me explain why I thought she was struggling and what we could do about it. Dweck's (2015) words bolstered me to say to her, "It seems to me that when you read, you often misinterpret the underlying meaning and the overall message." I provided her with examples from her work across texts. Then we talked about what strategies she could use to improve, and how I could help her. Dweck (2015) expresses, "It is about telling the truth about a student's current achievement and then, together, doing something about it, helping him or her become smarter." To have difficult conversations, teachers and students must have relationships built on mutual respect and trust so teachers can offer the feedback students need to succeed.

My science teacher—she treats me normal even though she knows that in sixth grade I had really bad grades. Now, because of her, I have good grades. —Seventh grader

I've had students approach me about grades and question my judgment using a less-than-optimal tone and approach. Since our relationship extends beyond grades and coursework, I can say to them, "Hey, let's back up a moment. I'm happy to talk to you about this, but please consider your approach and how that might have felt to me." And then we start the conversation from there.

Relationships and Connection

Relationships create the opening for students to share details about their lives that help teachers support them both academically and emotionally. One student revealed she could relate to a character in a novel who didn't have a mom. I thought to myself, "I didn't know she didn't have a mother!" However, to her, I said, "How do you feel you can relate to this character?" My student said, "My mom works a lot, and even when she's home, it's like she's still at work. Sometimes I feel like I don't have a home, and it feels very lonely." When I could catch my breath, I told her that although writing about her experience wouldn't change it, often writing and sharing our stories can lighten the burden and make us feel a little less lonely. (I also reached out to her guidance counselor, so she could get additional support.) Prior to this conversation, I didn't know this student very well, and her behavior was often hard to manage. Fortunately, this new understanding enabled me to better support her, and her classwork markedly improved.

These are the conversations I want to have with my students. These are the real lessons that will help them in their lives. There will always be content to teach, and content matters. But if we work together to build understanding in meaningful contexts, our students can apply the lessons they learn in school to new situations and transfer those skills beyond the classroom. The novelist and Pulitzer Prize–winning author Elizabeth Strout (as cited in Begley, 2017) writes, ". . . inside every person is a universe . . . and we'll never know what it feels like to be another person." I think, as teachers, we need to try to understand even a little bit about the "solar systems and galaxies" entrusted to us; and in turn, we can help students become acquainted with this "universe" that is uniquely their own as they seek to find their place in the world.

My band teacher taught me that no matter what happens in life, you have to keep your head up high. I've learned so much just from this one year. —Twelfth grader

Questions for Reflection

Consider these questions after reading the chapter.

If my students describe me as a teacher, how would they describe me? How would I want them to describe me? What changes might I need to make to be the teacher I want to be?

____

____

What understandings about teaching and learning do I currently use to guide my planning decisions?

____

____

What new understandings did I gain from this chapter, and how might I use this knowledge to improve my practice?

____

____

Who is this miracle speaking to me?
And who is this miracle listening?
What amazingness are we creating?
—Marilyn Nelson

Creating Relationships With Students

When I discussed my ideas for this book with a colleague, he shared reflections from a notebook he had kept early in his teaching career with me:

> 12.23.92—Connections. Trust. Respect. Students have to believe that you really care about them and the subject matter. Show them that you are there for them, and not them for you. You build relationships in the classroom. They have to trust you in order to speak out. Many have to be motivated by you, wanting to do well because it's interesting and because they want to do well for you and soon that will transfer to wanting to do well for themselves. (M. Wise, personal communication, July 26, 2018)

As soon as he finished reading, I responded, "You couldn't have written that in 1992! I invented that in 2018!" We laughed, because this is not true, of course. He continued: "I was overwhelmed at the beginning, but I've slowly got my head above water. I'm doing some good lessons and some lousy ones. I definitely need to improve and get less teacher-centric" (M. Wise, personal communication, July 26, 2018).

Although he clearly understood long ago the connection between relationships and learning, he never once invalidated the notion that I could add something new and worthwhile to the conversation. It is supportive relationships like these, with like-minded colleagues who not only don't begrudge our ideas but also generously share their own thoughts, that nurture us as teachers. These kinds of relationships mirror the relationships teachers should establish with students.

A study from the University of Chicago (as cited in Allensworth et al., 2018) notes, "Teachers' responsibilities have gone from managing students through a prescribed curriculum at a set pace, to creating the conditions and building the relationships that can nurture each student's social, emotional and academic development" (p. 2). It is (and always has been) true that strong teacher-student relationships positively impact learning outcomes and have the capacity to change the trajectory of students' lives (Rolland, 2012). Relationships with students have always mattered—long before the internet and social media, and regardless of whether teachers were writing on chalkboards or SMART Boards, or if students were writing in composition notebooks or on Google Docs.

Teachers carefully curate what they share with students, and how and when they interact with them, as well as how often. For some, this balance occurs more naturally, but for others it's helpful to have strategies, know what this looks like, and adapt it to what makes them feel comfortable. Some students make it easy to establish relationships with teachers, yet others can sit in class an entire school year and never reveal a sense of who they are.

What strategies can teachers use to forge meaningful relationships with their students? We can begin relating on the first day of school, try hard to set the tone during the first five days of the new year, establish expectations, show credibility, offer an invitation and an open chair, provide feedback, listen, foster student agency, take care of ourselves, avoid punitive practices, stand up for students, model the behavior we want to see, empathize, acknowledge our own imperfections, show warmth, and partner with parents.

Begin on the First Day of School

The choices teachers make during the first few weeks of school are critical and set the class tone for the entire year. Getting to know students, making them feel integral to the work we are doing together, and reassuring parents their children are safe in our class not only as learners but also as people, establish the foundation that enables us, as teachers, to meaningfully impact student learning.

My ninth graders arrive the first week anxious about high school and concerned about their appearance as they wander around the halls, schedules in hand, looking for their classrooms, desperately trying to arrive before the bell rings. It is essential on the first day of school for teachers to show students their classroom is a place students can rely on to feel safe and supported.

The best relationship that I have had with a teacher was with my second-grade teacher. She made me feel excited about school every day, and made me feel safe and most of all feel like I mattered. She was like a mother to me but in school. —Ninth grader

In her 2013 TED Talk, Rita Pierson (2013), a professional educator who followed both her parents' and grandparents' career path as an educator, says, "Kids don't learn from people they don't like." So, be someone your students will like. Create a classroom students want to come to. Let your students know they matter on the very first day. Pierson (2013) also says, "Some people think that you either have it in you to build a relationship or you don't." This is, of course, not true. Building strong relationships and creating a classroom where students feel they belong do not mean you are choosing to forgo challenging academics. Instead, it is the foundational piece teachers create to support the demands of the content and cushion the fall when students make mistakes; it is by design—your design.

If you want to jump into the curriculum the very first day, you can thread this foundational piece through your content introduction. My colleague, who distributes the class novel on the first day, is a teacher whose students love to be in her class, just love to be in her presence. Her class is not easy, but her students well know she designs the work to challenge them primarily because she cares so much about them. And when their grades falter and their confidence wavers, they know they can talk to her. Students can count on her to soothe and encourage, but they also know she will tell them the truth. When students feel connected to you and that they matter to you not only as learners but also as people, it opens up possibilities. Suddenly, distributing textbooks feels OK on the first day, as does assigning homework because students know it is purposeful and designed to move them forward toward the learning goals.

On the first day in my class, I may not distribute the class novel, but it's still not all stickers and smiley faces. My students arrive the first day to find assigned seats. As soon as they are settled, I explain how this seating arrangement helps me learn their names, and that these seats help us attend to the important work we need to do. I reassure them they can let me know if their seat is somehow problematic, but to be aware that we will have newly assigned seats each quarter.

Then, I introduce myself. I tell them they will meet many new teachers today, but when they think of me, they can remember these words from author, journalist, and columnist Anna Quindlen (2000) I write on the board: "I show up. I listen. I try to laugh" (p. 15).

Then I break it down for students.

- I tell them I will always show up for them, which doesn't mean I will never be absent, but if I am, there will be a post in Google Classroom (https://classroom.google.com), a Remind app text (https://remind.com), or they can reach me via email and hear back within twenty-four hours.
- I tell them I will always listen to them, and if they have a question, problem, or concern, they can always talk to me. Although I may not always agree with their point of view, I will always listen and consider what they have to say.
- I tell them since I also come to school every day, wherever possible, we will try to have fun and laugh as much as possible in the course of doing our important work.

I think this structure, coupled with my reassurances, makes them feel safe and supported, and it eases the path for us to tackle the hard work that lies ahead. Researchers Robert A. Hahn and Benedict I. Truman (2015, as cited in Robinson, Leeb, Merrick, & Forbes, 2016) explain that:

> optimal child development, health, and well-being depend on a foundation of safe, stable, and nurturing relationships and environments. The quality of this early foundation . . . has important implications for future learning, behavior, health and quality of life outcomes.

It follows that, "Because of the quantity of time children spend in school and the long term impacts of school related outcomes, the school ecology is a critical developmental context affecting not only their academic outcomes, but also their overall health" (Robinson et al., 2016).

There is always the temptation to discuss rules and policies the first day of school. However, if students arrive to a well-ordered class, I think it's enough to mention yours is a class that comes with rules, but policies are way too much to entirely absorb on your first day together. I do want them to know mine is a serious class, but I empathize with them how draining the first day can be.

Set the Tone During the First Five Days

After the first class, the rest of the week—the first five days—I primarily focus on building relationships and a sense of belonging as I slowly weave through the content, rules, and expectations. The balance for me shifts during these first five days, as my learning objectives and the course content rise closer to the forefront as the days progress.

My favorite beginning-of-the-year activity—I assign it on the first day of school—is called #freshmanyear (figure 2.1). It includes each student's picture and some personal details they choose to share. I assign a template through Google

Classroom for students to customize, and I provide models of previous students' work, as well as one of my own. As the assignment requires students to compose a six-word memoir, we view a few short YouTube videos (like the one at https://bit.ly/2SOYbcf) of teenagers sharing their six words. Students submit this assignment through Google Classroom and print their work in color to hang on a clothesline around the classroom, where their work remains for the entire school year.

Directions: Personalize this document by completing the following information. Please print this in color. We will display the work in our classroom for the entire school year. Express your creativity with the font and colors you choose, as well as the picture you share with us!

My name is ____.

One quotation that best expresses one of my philosophies on life is

____.

My best family memory is ______________________________

____.

An item on my wish list or in my shopping cart is ______________

____.

My favorite book or author is ____________________________.

My best trait is______________________________________.

My dream job is _____________________________________.

I am most proud of ___________________________________.

My six-word memoir is ________________________________

____.

Insert Your Photo Here

Figure 2.1: The #freshmanyear template.

Visit **go.SolutionTree.com/literacy** for a free reproducible version of this figure.

On the day the assignment is due, students take a clothespin, come to the front of the room, and share their name and memoir. Each student says, "My name is ____________________ and my six-word memoir is ____________________ ____________________." As students hang up their work, our classroom becomes a reflection of the community we are building. The other details on #freshmanyear become conversations during the remainder of the year, as students are constantly drawn to look at one another's pictures and read their words.

My fifth-grade teacher treated us almost not like students and ten-year-olds, but instead as adults and peers. I don't really remember what type of math or what time period in history she taught, but I remember the friendships I formed and the bond I had with her. —Ninth grader

---

During the last week of school, I ask students to write another six-word memoir, and on the last day, students take down their #freshmanyear assignment, read their memoir from the beginning of the year, and share their memoir for the end of the year. It feels a little bit like bringing our time together full circle. Author Daniel H. Pink (2018) likes this idea so much, he includes it in his book, *When: The Scientific Secrets of Perfect Timing*. Pink (2018) writes, "At the end of a school term, many students feel a sense of relief. But with a little thought and planning, they can also experience a sense of elevation" (p. 172). A classroom that is a visual reflection of its learners is a constant reminder that it is their presence and their voices that drive the work.

This activity extends beyond building relationships and establishing a sense of belonging. It provides an opportunity for me to get to know my students and allows me to assess their evident strengths, as well as introduce classroom routines. On the day students present their #freshmanyear assignment, I explain how we will snap our fingers in support of one another when students present in front of the room, and throughout the year, we will snap our fingers whenever we want to acknowledge one another and show our appreciation. I remind them that snapping fingers says, "We're listening, and what you say matters to us." It's not, "You did a great job." It's, "You did it, and we're here for you."

The thrum of snapping fingers sets a supportive tone for the class. As the weeks progress, I snap when a student asks a question others might perceive as not worth asking. I'll then say, "Thank you for being brave enough to ask that question. I'm sure many others had the same question." We also snap fingers when a student makes a particularly insightful remark and even when someone is stumbling nervously through a presentation. Sometimes I forget to snap when one of my students needs encouragement, but I'll often hear some quiet snaps from the back of the room.

Another way to get to know students and show I value them is when they make remarks or share bits of insight that pique my curiosity. I ask them questions: "OK, so you're the third student to tell me about K-Pop. Who can send me a video to see what the big deal is?" I've also learned a little more about Vines, dad jokes, popular Netflix series, and YouTubers who are making a career out of things I've yet to completely understand. Listening to and learning about students' interests provides the basis for conversation. It also infuses a level of excitement into the class, as students eagerly provide updates; they know I'm listening. As author and educator Gillian Parrish (as cited in Steen, 2017a) states, "As teachers we are not just presenting information. . . . We need to genuinely value students' voices, allowing their questions and ideas to inform the moment for everyone."

The rhythm of the first five days continues to evolve as the students engage and I learn about new ideas, consider student shares and feedback, and continually reevaluate and readjust. Generally, the first five days are a mash-up of icebreakers, name games, supply checks, and Google Classroom sign ups, with the slow unfolding of rules, expectations, and content. In my class, as everyone gets to know one another, students read about reading (to rediscover why we all read), brush up on their writing skills (to preassess), and get comfortable speaking in front of the class (so I can hear their voices and learn their names). The plan is that by day six, their binder tabs are labelled, I'm calling many by their first names, I'm sprinkling in rules, and I'm still working on building that solid foundation. Yet mine is a ninth-grade honors course, so the class is also discussing the Trojan War and diving into *The Odyssey*—unabridged (Homer, 8th century BC/1999).

During the third or fourth week of school, once I feel students have a sense of who I am (and I comfortably know their names), I ask them to write, in one sentence on an index card, something they'd like me to know about them. When I read these cards, I test myself to see if I can picture each face as I read his or her words. These index cards are quick to read and easy to store for the entire school year in case I want to refer back to them. Teachers can, of course, do this using Google Classroom questions, Google Forms (https://google.com/forms/about), or the like. Personally, I like to get to see my students' handwriting, and these shares seem more personal when students hand them to me and when I hold them in my hands. Regardless, it is important for teachers to figure out how to get to know students in a manageable way; I think it's equally important for students to understand how much we want to know them.

Establish Expectations

One of the first pieces of advice I received as a new teacher was to solidly establish my expectations and set the tone for my classroom before diving into content. (I try to remember this advice as my chest tightens at visions of me distributing class novels on the first day of school.) Another helpful philosophy I learned was, in the words of Willard R. Daggett (2015), president of the International Center for Leadership in Education, the three Rs: rigor, relevance, and relationship. Although my understanding of Daggett's (2015) philosophy was a bit simplistic then, I clung to these guidelines as I continually asked myself these questions.

- "Is the work challenging enough?"
- "Is the work relevant to my students' lives?"
- "What am I doing to establish meaningful relationships with my students?"

My first-grade teacher positively impacted my life when she would contact my parents weekly about how I was doing since she knew I was having challenges at home. She showed me not only family members can love you. —Ninth grader

---

Show Credibility

Unconsciously, students spend the first five days assessing who their teachers are—what we are about, what we have to offer them, and how they will likely feel about our class. We can use this time to subtly convey evidence of our credibility, which coauthors Douglas Fisher and Nancy Frey (2018) explain "has a strong effect size on student learning . . . twice the impact on learning that student motivation does" per Hattie (2012). Students need to immediately recognize that teachers have something of value to offer them so they will truly invest their time and energy in class. "If a teacher is not perceived as credible, the students just turn off" (Hattie, 2012, as cited in Fisher & Frey, 2018). Fisher and Frey (2018) indicate four components of teacher credibility, and I've adapted their work with questions and suggestions to consider how teachers can intentionally demonstrate their credibility to students.

1. **Competence:** Clearly demonstrate your understanding of the subject matter. Students should know *what* they're learning—and, more important, *why* they're learning it.
2. **Immediacy:** Show students you will partner with them in the learning process. Get out from behind your desk and sit in a circle with students. Pull up a chair to join their groups. Offer them the front of the room while you sit in the back and listen.
3. **Dynamism:** Share your passion for your subject. Are you an English teacher who's also a writer? Are you a science teacher who keeps reptiles as pets? Are you a history teacher who's active in local politics?
4. **Trust:** Listen to students and be responsive to their needs. Be consistent. Abide by rules you establish. Be available for questions. Let students know you care about them and their ability to succeed.

If you are designing with the end in mind, you can consider not only lessons and activities for the first five days, but prepared remarks, the seating arrangement, and planned interactions with students to ensure you are clearly establishing your credibility and creating a solid foundation designed to support you and your students for the rest of the school year.

In seventh grade, I had a science teacher who would make sure every single student in the class understood what we were doing. She would go around to each table to help anyone that was confused, and I was not afraid to ask questions because she never judged if your question was maybe not the smartest question. —Ninth grader

---

Offer an Invitation and an Open Chair

In my language arts classroom, one of my main challenges is to help students become better writers. Many students struggle to construct sentences, develop compelling arguments, and advance from basic plot summary to critical text analysis. So, I keep a chair with the seat facing me next to my desk. That way, when students are working, this chair is available to them to come up and ask me questions.

When students approach my desk, often standing at first, I encourage them to sit down. I often read aloud their words to them. When students hear their words read aloud, it helps them quickly identify their mistakes. But their writing is sometimes painful for them to hear, so I try to do this in myriad ways without causing them shame and embarrassment. Brown (2013) defines shame as the "intensely painful feeling or experience of believing we are flawed and therefore unworthy of love and belonging—something we've experienced, done, or failed to do makes us unworthy of connection" (p. 5). We must be careful, because causing shame will damage the trust and connection we are trying so hard to build with students. Sometimes, this is done with one part criticism and two parts humor, and sometimes with an "empathy sandwich:" "I really liked this part, but then when you wrote . . ." "It gave me chills when you said . . . " "It was confusing when . . . " Other times, I ooze compassion as I read their words to them, and say, "I know you wrote that. How does it sound now that I'm reading it back to you?"

Fifth grade is very complicated, but on the first day of school, when the teacher started to tell us a little bit about himself, I knew that fifth grade would be awesome! —Fifth grader

---

We need students to feel comfortable with us and motivated to enter into the messy work of learning. We need them to want to come up and sit in the empty chair to ask questions even when it still makes them a little uneasy. As coauthors Jay McTighe and Judy Willis (2019) write, "Effective teachers recognize that if they care about students' academic learning, they must also be attentive to the social and emotional factors that affect their learners" (p. 139).

Provide Feedback

Student feedback has been instrumental in helping me shape my instructional strategies. I consistently offer students time to offer me feedback throughout the school year as well as at the end of the year (usually on a Google Form; figure 2.2). This feedback serves two purposes: (1) I get important information about my class and (2) it conveys to my students that I care what they think.

As I implement their feedback, it reinforces to students that they matter to me, and we are in this together. Sometimes it's too late to respond meaningfully to student feedback (as with the end-of-the-year template), and other times I learn more about myself and my class than I want to hear. But the feedback is still valuable as I make revisions to create a better experience for future students. And every year, this is exactly what I try to do.

I'd like to tell you the longer you teach, the water will get clearer, and sometimes it will. There will be triumphs and moments of elation, and you'll think, "I've finally got this!" But then more sediment will rise from the bottom and the water will become increasingly murky as students arrive with new challenges, and federal and state mandates require changes that don't seem to make sense. Since we often can't see the way ahead, we need to look at who's right in front of us, embrace the uncertainty, make the best decisions we can, and continually reflect, re-evaluate, and adjust. There is power in admitting that you don't have all of the answers; it can inspire you to ask different questions and perhaps find new solutions.

My eighth-grade science teacher is the reason that I found my passion for medicine. She was a teacher who demanded a lot from each student. She was always encouraging and kind, and available to listen. I still update her every few months about my life, and she continues to inspire me every day. —Ninth grader

---

Name: ____

Directions: Please answer each question honestly and explain your response fully. It will help improve the experience for future students in this class.

1. What assignment or activity this year taught you the most or was the most rewarding?

   ____
   ____
   ____

2. What assignment or activity this year was the least worthwhile for you?

   ____
   ____
   ____

3. What do you wish we, as a class, would do more of or less of? Why?

   ____
   ____
   ____

4. How did the classroom environment affect your performance in this class?

   ____
   ____
   ____

5. Did you feel the grading in this class was too hard, too easy, or just right? What could I do to make this better for future students?

   ____
   ____
   ____

6. What was the most important lesson you learned this year, or what skill do you think improved the most as a result of this class?

   ____
   ____
   ____

Figure 2.2: End-of-the-year feedback template.

Visit **go.SolutionTree.com/literacy** for a free reproducible version of this figure.

My story is not over; it is a continual beginning. Our teaching story evolves as our students change, standardized tests create new demands, districts institute new policies, and curricula change in response. As teachers, we need to remain focused on what is working and not working for students, as we continually ask ourselves: "How are my students going to learn what they need to know to be fully prepared for their lives beyond school?"

In so many ways, I think our students have these answers. They know what will capture their attention, what problems they need to solve, what questions they want answered, what they most want to express, who they want to be, and how they want to be seen by the world. I think the invitation is to arrive to school every day eternally curious, with our ears pressed to the din of our students' voices as we learn and listen with *our pens in the air* (Oliver, 2016).

Listen

If we listen closely to students, their words can guide us toward ways we can engage them so they become more conscientious readers, effective writers, confident speakers, and empathic listeners. Parrish (as cited in Steen, 2017b) writes, "The effect of a good listener on student learning is electrifying. When students are heard, when their insights strike their listener, when their questions open up discussions, when their ideas are taken up and explored sincerely, then they blossom." It seems to me it's time to "reconsider the old notion that students must be quiet and listen to their teachers" (Pandolpho, 2018a). Maybe it's time for teachers to be quiet and listen to them. That way, we can get to know students, be responsive, ask for feedback, and remember things they've told us, in conferences and beyond.

Get to Know Them

During the first week of school, I used to distribute a double-sided handout titled Getting to Know You. To me, it communicated: "I care about you!" and "I want to know you!" But at the beginning of the school year, when I didn't yet know the students' names, it almost rendered their answers meaningless. I decided to hold on to them and not read them until I had learned my students' names.

My fourth-grade teacher taught me the most because she taught me to believe in myself. —Fifth grader

---

This solution proved a bit more successful until one year when I didn't remove the handouts from my grading folder until early October (much to my embarrassment). And then my eyes glazed over as I read many responses that made me feel like I didn't know anybody any better. "I like dogs." "I like teachers who show they care." "My favorite Netflix series is *Stranger Things*." I knew I needed to do something more. Educator, consultant, and author Rick Wormeli (2016) writes:

> Although we can build positive relationships throughout the school year, the first weeks are crucial. They set the tone and conditions for the year ahead, creating a more effective teaching and learning enterprise for everyone. James Comer, professor of child psychiatry at Yale University, often declares, "No significant learning can occur without a significant relationship."

I realized I needed to make a bigger push to get to know students' first names as soon as possible. So, in September I do icebreakers such as Two Truths and One Lie and Stand Up Sit Down. I've had students produce short book talk videos about their summer reading and thirty-second introductions for which they design their own slide on an editable Google Slides (https://google.com/slides/about) presentation. A fun twist during these activities is I tell students to be prepared to answer questions if their response piques my curiosity. Some students see this as a challenge, others hope I won't ask, but overall almost everyone likes to talk about themselves. All of these activities take time and each has its benefits, so I think teachers must decide exactly what they want to know and how much time they want to invest in finding out.

I like Stand Up Sit Down (adapted from For the Teachers, 2012) because it is interactive, gets students out of their seats, and helps me commit a few names to memory. (Once a student describes to you the first time eating a bug, you generally remember that student's name for the rest of the school year.)

I say a phrase like those listed here, and students stand to indicate *yes* (adapted from For the Teachers, 2012). They stay seated if their response is *no*. I let them know that if they are standing, I may ask them to tell me more about their yes.

- I am glad to be at school.
- I prefer summer more than winter.
- I have had stitches.
- I have a dog.
- I have a cat.
- I have the same first name as someone in your family.
- I cut my own hair.
- I have traveled out of the country.
- I have eaten a bug.
- I help with chores around the house.
- I have had a cavity.
- I have a reptile.
- I am related to someone famous.
- I speak more than one language.
- I have broken a bone.
- I don't care if my socks match.
- I have three or more pets.
- I play an instrument.

- I am tired.
- I would eat anything if it were covered in chocolate.
- I am a good singer.
- I play a sport.
- I have ridden a camel.
- I think I might like this class.

Be Responsive

On many days, my inbox is sprinkled with students' emails because I encourage students to email me if they have concerns. Generally, these emails contain requests to schedule a makeup exam, questions about an upcoming assignment, or inquiries about work missed as a result of absence. I assure my students their emails are not a bother, and if I can ease their concerns with a quick response from my phone, then I want to. Because these email exchanges are very personal connections with individual students, they build relationships.

The next day, when students approach my desk at the beginning of class, I already know about the upcoming model United Nations trip or that they are leaving school early for marching band because we were in touch the night before. During hectic moments, I'll give a knowing glance and a quick comment to reassure the student who emailed me, so I can then attend to the other twenty-five students who are ready for class to begin.

My students know I have a busy life, and I often email them back when I'm cooking dinner or attending my son's football game. They understand emails are not the forum for questions about grades or details that can wait until the following school day. They also know if I can ease their concerns or clarify any confusion, I want to.

At the beginning of the year, when a deadline is looming, or toward the end of a marking period, my inbox may be full. But when I consistently address concerns and assuage feelings, my students need me less and my inbox is lighter. I know many teachers who are not interested in receiving student emails when they are off the clock. But honestly, I find it rewarding to ease student concerns with a quick response from my phone. Also, from September through June, I never feel like I'm off the clock. I think about my students and my lesson plans all the time when I'm not at school, so these emails do not feel like an intrusion. Responding to student emails feels like part of the job to me, and my availability means a lot to them. My own children are proud of me because I respond to and take care of my students. They are grateful when they have teachers like me.

My fourth-grade teacher has taught me a lot of important things in life. She was gentle and understanding and looked after us. She helped us if we didn't understand what to do. —Fifth grader

---

I think being responsive to students' needs is a teaching opportunity; we are teaching students to advocate for themselves, and in response, they can expect us to treat them with kindness and respect. If a student has a conflict outside school that prohibits the timely completion of an assignment, offer an extension if the student coordinates in advance. If a student misunderstands the directions on an assignment and does poorly as a result, consider if it was an honest mistake. After all, school is preparation for life, and "school and life are about learning, not about getting it right the first time" (Pandolpho & Wise, 2018). Consider being the teacher who offers what Wormeli (2011) refers to as redos, retakes, and do-overs. You will quickly know which students are just offering excuses, and which students truly need support.

These individual exchanges not only forge stronger individual bonds, but also seep into the class culture as a whole. When class begins, my students give me their attention not simply because I am the teacher; they listen to me, in part, because I listen to them.

Ask for Feedback

If you ask students what they think, they will tell you. Because I've asked students for feedback, I know most of them appreciate that I don't give pop quizzes, but that they think my reading quizzes are too tough. I've learned that it helps to include the due date option in Google Classroom to send reminders, and although I dread using class time to return and review essays and quizzes, students tell me my feedback really helps.

My students know I'm doing the best I can, but because I'm not sitting at their desks, completing the homework, or juggling any other subjects, I can't possibly predict every possible outcome or be certain everything I do is objectively fair. The only way I can aspire to these goals is by inviting students to help me view the work from their perspective. Don't get me wrong—sometimes the feedback stings (really stings), but even as I wince, I am still usually glad I asked so I don't repeat the same mistakes. As students often must accept feedback they would rather not hear (generally in the form of a grade), this understanding emboldens me to ask for and accept the feedback my students so generously offer.

You can ask for quick comments on index cards as students leave class, offer targeted questions, have students discuss their responses in groups and submit anonymous feedback to you, or sit in a student desk and open the floor to a town meeting. Remember to set norms for feedback. Sometimes I ask very general questions: "How are things going for you in class?", "What am I missing?", or "What do you want me to know?" Other times they are very specific: "Is the reading schedule too much?" or "Do you need more guidance or time to prepare for the Socratic seminar?"

Remember

Remembering what students tell you and acting on it let them know you have been listening and what they say matters to you. Months after it was turned in, I reminded one student how I loved his essay about Toni Morrison's (1970) *The Bluest Eye*, for example. The prior year, a student performed an unforgettable dramatic interpretation of one of Romeo's monologues for our annual Shakespeare birthday celebration. When I ran into him in the hallway a year later, I reminded him and promptly recounted one of the highlights of his performance. He laughed in recognition and seemed genuinely surprised I remembered.

Conference With Them

Another way to ensure teachers connect with each student is through individual conferences. Conferences are something teachers absolutely don't have time for, but we must make time for—especially for those students we haven't yet connected with one-to-one, or who seem particularly reticent. The benefits of teacher-student conferencing far outweigh the use of class time. Admittedly, conferencing with students presents many challenges. What are the other students doing while the teacher is conferencing? How many days will it take for the teacher to meet with each student? How long should these conferences be? And, of course, the even larger question, What exactly are teachers doing in these conferences, and why are they doing it?

These questions are worth answering because a conference is a conversation. If teachers never conference, it is likely there will be students with whom they will never have a sustained conversation. A conference offers the opportunity to make eye contact, lean in, and convey, "I am here for you. How is it that I can best help you?" When my students sit down and we first look at each other, we usually begin by saying "hi" and then kind of sheepishly laugh with each other. It is surprisingly personal and sometimes a bit awkward to sit down individually with each student. And yet, these private moments lead to more critical conversations, and knowing more about students' lives, passions, and interests provides an opening to help teachers guide them to more meaningful learning tailored to their interests.

I sometimes build in miniconferences when I'm doing quick check-ins to assess progress and completion. I call students up individually to sit in the open chair next to my desk, and I write on the board what each needs to bring to show me. I tell each student that since I want to make the most of our time together, to please come prepared with conversation starters (figure 2.3). Most students love having my full attention as well as being in charge of the conversation. For me, the details I learn during these brief encounters offer me insight into students' lives that help me help them.

Directions: Choose two of the conversation starters to complete, so we can make the most of our time together!

One thing I'd like to ask you is ________________________________.

One thing I'd like to tell you about is ___________________________.

Something I'd like you to know is _______________________________.

One interesting thing that happened this week is _________________
____.

I'm most afraid of __________________ because __________________.

Lately I'm feeling worried about __________________ because
____.

One way you can help me is ____________________________________.

You might be surprised to know that ____________________________.

Something I wish we'd do more of in class is ______________________
because ___________________.

Lately I've been wondering ______________________ because
____.

Lately I've been feeling ______________________ because
____.

Figure 2.3: Conversation starters.

Visit **go.SolutionTree.com/literacy** for a free reproducible version of this figure.

Foster Student Agency

In addition to being responsive to students' emotional lives, teachers must motivate students beyond compliance and toward agency. Poet, essayist, and feminist Adrienne Rich said it best during a 1977 convocation at Douglass College: "You cannot afford to think of being here to receive an education; you will do much better to think of yourselves as being here to claim one." In my class, my students and I brainstorm about the kinds of things we claim, and the students make analogies to something they would reach out and grab or get up to collect. I remind them that the things we receive are like packages from Amazon and presents on our birthdays, but they can't sit back and be the recipient of an education through some kind of wireless router that enables me to transmit information, skills, and life lessons.

Teachers should enlist all efforts toward student engagement if they want students to develop as readers, writers, speakers, listeners, and thinkers. According to Darling-Hammond and Cook-Harvey (2018), "Personalizing the educational setting so that it responds to individual students' interests and needs, as well as their home and community contexts, is one of the most powerful levers to change the trajectories for children's lives" (p. 15). Students should be active participants in their own learning, and if teachers take the time to listen to them and learn about what motivates them, what interests them, what they are afraid of, and how they can help, teachers can use this information to design learning experiences that foster engagement.

According to the theory of self-determination, in order to foster agency, students need to connect with others and have a degree of autonomy and competence (Ryan & Deci, 2000). Although teachers are charged with covering curriculum and adhering to state and district mandates, we can still offer some kind of personalization, choice, and autonomy. We can follow all of the rules and guidelines and still focus more on our students. We don't need to define it as personalized learning, student-centered learning, or differentiation. Instead, in the spirit of UbD (Wiggins & McTighe, 2005), we can just call it teaching for understanding, which begins with finding the spark that will motivate each student, ignite his or her curiosity, and foster agency. When we listen, guide, and pay attention, it enables us to create a pathway for each student. It is then that our students will intuitively know we are not only there with them but also there for them. This is where learning begins.

I really don't have a specific teacher that made a difference in my life. All my teachers helped me throughout the years. If they didn't, I wouldn't be where I am today. —Twelfth grader

---

A more student-focused learning environment built on strong relationships and belonging fosters engagement, so students will immerse themselves in the repeated practice necessary to master the requisite content and skills they need for their lives beyond our classroom (Pink, 2014, as cited in Azzam, 2014).

Just as we can't make people follow our advice or solve anyone else's problem, teachers can't just teach and expect students to learn. The only lasting change results from what people can do for themselves, and the only learning that students can do must occur as a result of their own actions. Teachers know this. As Wormeli (2016) writes, "When we affirm to each student, 'Yes, you exist; I accept all that you are, and I value time in your company,' it opens the door to the successful teaching-learning dynamic so important to academic success." Wiggins (2014) reminds us, "the only hope for significant advancement of engagement and thus performance is to spend each day in a joyful, focused, and collaborative school. That's what the data say; that's what common sense says." No lecture, technology tool, standardized test, online learning platform, or teacher observation system is going to advance student learning more powerfully and effectively than relationships, belonging, and personalized learning. By listening to our students, we are in turn teaching them how to listen to themselves.

Take Care of Yourself

It's very easy to become mired in ungraded papers and an inbox brimming with unanswered emails, wondering if the copy machine will still be jammed next free period and what to do if it is. I'm often distracted by looming faculty meetings, book orders that may or may not have arrived, and upcoming schedule changes designed to accommodate standardized tests, assemblies, and pep rallies. I try to remind myself that there will be days I will get some work done at school, but there will be many more days when my job in the classroom is to simply be present for my students.

So, I conference with students during lunch and free periods, write recommendations for summer programs and college, and field requests to read the first one hundred pages of the novel a student wrote. Students ask me to buy cookie dough, raffle tickets, and Girl Scout cookies, and can I chaperone bingo on a Friday night, judge a spelling bee on Saturday, and attend the science fair on Sunday? It is often difficult to prioritize this influx of requests, because sometimes the cookie dough purchase from a particular student will pay relationship dividends that last throughout the school year. And at other times, giving up my weekend is simply more than I can manage.

In the midst of caring for my students, I try to remember that it's OK to say no. I try to say yes to the requests that meet a particular student's needs or that feel manageable to me. This protects the teacher-student relationship. University of Missouri College of Education professor Keith Herman cautions: "When stress interferes with personal and emotional well-being at such a severe level, the relationships teachers have with students are likely to suffer" (as cited in Riley-Missouri, 2018).

When I do say no to students, I try to explain why. I want them to understand that if I say no to their requests, I am saying yes to myself. And although the no is not what they want to hear, I hope they can learn from my example. I am modeling self-care. Self-care author Tina H. Boogren (2018) reminds teachers:

> Research-based educational strategies and pedagogy are only as good as the person providing them. And if the human providing the strategies is so depleted, worn out and burned out that he or she can hardly breathe, then the expectation that he or she can provide oxygen to students is unrealistic. (p. 4)

This is how teachers can show up for students, and these intentional moves build relationships. Perfect attendance at meetings and quick turnaround grading times are meaningless if we're not present for our students.

Avoid Punitive Practices

It is worth remembering to be cautious about practices that can damage or sever teacher-student relationships. Punishment (versus discipline) is harmful to relationships and learning (Banfield, Richmond, & McCroskey, 2006). In fact, a "non-threatening learning environment develops a sense of belonging among students" (Freeman, Anderman, & Jensen, 2007). If a large majority of your class doesn't submit an assignment, before entering zeros into the online gradebook, ask yourself, "Was I clear enough in my instructions? Why did so many students fail to submit the assignment?" When you aren't receiving responses during a whole-class discussion and it seems many students aren't paying attention, before catching students unaware, consider saying, "I see many of you aren't with me. Take a few minutes to look at your notes and talk to the people sitting next to you. After that, it seems fair to call on people at random to answer my questions."

It is very easy to turn students off with an unfair grade, an embarrassing moment, or a throwaway remark.

Stand Up for Them

When my class discusses controversial issues or elements worthy of argument or further discussion, I'm a big fan of the Four Corners activity. I like to do this activity further into the year, or once students have participated in lower-stakes speaking opportunities and feel more comfortable voicing their opinions. In most of my Four Corners activities, students read to themselves a list of debatable statements and decide whether they strongly agree, agree, disagree, or strongly disagree. After they've marked a response for each of these statements, I read the statements and students move to the labeled corner of the room that matches their opinion. I give them time in their corner to discuss how and why they reached their decision with other like-minded students in their corner before organizing dialogues between students in each of the corners.

The activity never fails to bring a new energy to the class. Students get to be on their feet, move around the room, and stand with like-minded peers. They get the rare opportunity to speak loudly (so students on the other side of the room can hear them), and they are more likely to participate because other class members support them—they are literally in their corner. Also, "by creating a rich contextual environment, kinesthetic learning constructs memories connected to time, place, and emotions, which we call episodic encoding. Students activate and integrate physical, emotional, and cognitive responses to what they are learning, making learning more meaningful" (Griss, 2013). I generally stand in the center as the conversation facilitator to ensure each student gets to share his or her voice and to encourage spirited, yet civil dialogue.

I do tell students there's a chance they might find themselves alone in a corner. They may be alone in their views or find they hold an unpopular opinion. However, I insist they committedly walk to the corner representative of their opinion, and assure them that if they are alone in a corner, I will stand with them whether I am in agreement or not.

I had a surprising moment during Four Corners while students were prereading Elie Wiesel's (1960/2006) *Night*. I distributed a handout from the U.S. Holocaust Memorial Museum (USHMM, n.d.) titled "Assessing and Defining Responsibility." The handout asks students to think about who was responsible for the events between 1933 and 1945. One of the statements reads, "A person who turned the lever to allow the gas into the chambers" was "not responsible" to "very responsible" (USHMM, n.d., p. 2). One of my students walked alone to the "not responsible" corner while other students watched aghast. As promised, I walked over and stood next to the student.

The Four Corners activity doesn't always have to involve controversy; it also works well as an icebreaker at the beginning of the year. Figure 2.4 is a handout that works well at the beginning of the year. Since the activity feels less like a traditional classroom discussion, it often leads to deeper insights and more thoughtful conversations. It also offers teachers (and students) the unique opportunity to demonstrate respect for others' opinions.

Directions: Stand in the corner that represents what makes you the most uncomfortable.

- Sharing an unpopular opinion
- Asking for help
- Standing up for yourself
- Trying something new

Share with the peers in your corner an example of a situation when this would make you feel uncomfortable.

Source: Adapted from Andrea Bean & Susan Totaro, West Windsor-Plainsboro Regional School District, 2019.

Figure 2.4: Four Corners activity example.

Visit **go.SolutionTree.com/literacy** for a free reproducible version of this figure.

You can extend this activity or use it as an icebreaker to get further information about how to meet your students' needs by asking them to think about and discuss a favorite teacher with the others in their corner. Then, ask them to reflect on how this teacher helped them overcome an obstacle or helped them feel more at ease. Students love sharing anecdotes about favorite teachers with their classmates in the corners. You'll likely hear overlapping stories and common themes that can help inform the choices you make in your classroom.

Model the Behavior You Want to See

Students are forever watching and listening to teachers. From the moment we walk into the school building to the stories we share about our lives outside school, they are conducting an analysis of our character, even if it's not entirely accurate. Our words and actions are consequential, so teachers need to be mindful to model the kind of behavior we'd like to see from students. Author Michael Sadowski (2013) cites psychologist Jean E. Rhodes, who documents:

> The potential for 'naturally occurring mentoring relationships'—such as those that students can have with teachers . . . to make a profound difference in the lives of adolescents, provided they are of sufficient duration and are marked by key characteristics, such as consistency and empathy.

Modeling happens both inside and outside the classroom.

In the Classroom

As teachers, we plan lessons, create seating arrangements, and choose when students can and can't talk. We assign homework and grades, and even decide whether or not students are allowed to go to the bathroom or get a drink of water. Teachers expect respectful behavior and active listening, and personally I insist phones be out of sight. I work hard to abide by the same guidelines and expectations I set for my students and model fairness, compassion, and humility.

For example, if a student submits a late assignment on the heels of my returning quizzes after a considerable length of time, I might accept it without deducting points and say, "You know, I was really late getting those quizzes back to you, so I understand what it feels like to fall behind." And whenever possible, I invite students into my "teacher brain" to share what it looks like to do this job. I tell students when I'm grading their papers, I am sifting through a pile of over one hundred papers. I try to remain focused and yet still, I make mistakes. I may miss something. So if students think they notice an error or want to talk to me about a grade or concern they have, I welcome the conversation. I remind students that I may not always agree, but we can talk about it. Often, being heard is enough.

I want students to value our class time, so I try to use our time together wisely. If there isn't anything specific they need to do to prepare for our next class, I don't manufacture homework. I'm sure their other teachers have assigned homework, and I know my students are plenty busy.

I own my limitations, and I apologize for my mistakes. I acknowledge that while their phones are to be kept out of sight, mine is visible on my desk. I explain that I have children, and sometimes other teachers text me about things they need during the school day. It is a double standard, of course, but I want them to know the reasons. I like to think of myself as director of learning rather than the person in charge, and model the behavior I want to see. Modeling behavior is a powerful agent of change. Psychologist and Stanford University professor Albert Bandura's (1977) book *Social Learning Theory* states, "Fortunately, most human behavior is learned observationally through modeling: from observing others one forms an idea of how new behaviors are performed, and on later occasions this coded information serves as a guide for action" (p. 22).

Outside the Classroom

I encourage my students to take risks—to volunteer to speak in class even when they feel self-conscious and are afraid of being wrong. Remember, I tell them, "Pushing yourself out of your comfort zone is how you grow!" I continue, "I want to hear some voices I haven't heard recently. Here is the question I am going to ask, and I'm going to give you a few minutes to write about it, and then talk it through with your group. After that, I will feel everyone is prepared, so I might call on you. You can read directly from what you wrote, or you can frame your response like this . . . ." (Sometimes I'll write an opening phrase on the board for quick reference.) For painfully shy students, I may walk over while they are thinking out their responses and quietly say, "I'd like to hear your voice today. Will it completely ruin your day if I call on you?" I've yet to have a student decline.

I like to think my students take risks because I model this same kind of risk taking. In 2018, I participated in a teacher dance with our South Asian American Student Association (SAASA) in front of a sold-out crowd; I was barefoot and wearing bangles and a dupatta. Learning the steps was a challenge to me, and I wasn't very good. My students know following along in an exercise class or clapping in time with music is difficult for me, and I was always the last person chosen for a team in physical education. But in our school, SAASA is the biggest event of the year, and I wanted to step into my students' world the way they so graciously step into mine.

Empathize

My students care about grades—a lot. Students care about grades because they matter in the world. I get it, but students care so much about their grades sometimes I wonder if they even care if they learn anything. Often during class, I find students distractedly looking at our online grading portal. I tell them there is nothing to learn there and say, "Come back to us."

The very existence of grades sets up an adversarial relationship between teachers and students. Students feel judged, measured, and evaluated as people; their feelings are hurt, and it feels like teachers are the ones who are hurting them. Wormeli (2018a) cautions teachers, "conventional grading practices [can] undermine students' learning and our system of schooling." Yet, grades are a part of the imperfect system we call school, so teachers need to carefully leverage the reality of grades in terms of nurturing relationships.

My students know grading and assigning grades are my least favorite part of the job. They know if I was really in charge, there would be all feedback and no grades. They know I care about learning, not grades, and I only care about grades to the extent they do. I try to neutralize the impact of grades by being transparent about what I'm grading, how much it counts, how I decide on the percentage, and why I think it's an important assessment. I don't give surprise quizzes, and students will never get a gotcha from me. Grades are information about a student's performance and, if teachers grade wisely, an indicator of their ability. However, we need to be mindful; grades have the power to negatively impact student learning, but we, as teachers, have the power to ensure they don't.

Acknowledge Your Imperfections

I think, as teachers, we need to not be afraid to show our vulnerability because this is the only way for students to understand we also feel insecure and uncertain at times. Vulnerability is also a precursor to building a relationship. I try to model for my students through my teaching practice and lesson design that it is not only courageous to be vulnerable, but also that allowing yourself to be seen by another person is how you create the space for a relationship to begin. As ethics professor and researcher Christine Straehle (2014) notes, "For most, the vulnerability that comes with relationships is something we accept; we risk getting into relationships, because the promise of our emotional gains outweighs the risk of having our interests harmed" (p. 199).

I've shared with my students that I was always the second-to-last kid picked for a team in gym class, and I was only second-to-last because other kids liked me—not because I wasn't clearly the worst athlete. I've confided that as an adult, I stand in the back of my exercise class because I have a hard time moving my hands and feet in time with the music. My students know that the only reason their grade calculations are accurate is because our grading portal does all of the calculations for me and that if they toss me a dry erase marker, I am unlikely to catch it.

Our students need to know that as much as we are different, we are also very much the same. Our students need to know that although we appear before them with many answers, there is no such thing as having all the answers. I remind them that one of the secrets to life is finding a job that you love and that you're good at. It is the reason I'm not a gym teacher or an accountant. Teachers can show students in these small ways that we are in this with them—not only this thing called school, but this thing called life.

Show Warmth

Hattie (2012) reminds us, "teachers must show warmth in observable ways rather than simply intend to do so or believe that it is important" (p. 140). But since there is no one right way to do this, each teacher needs to show this love in his or her own ways. When we radiate warmth, we draw other people to us. When teachers visibly care for students, students seek out those teachers for mentoring, knowledge, feedback, and support. One colleague stands in the hallway and greets her students as they enter her classroom every single day. Another colleague hasn't eaten lunch with other teachers in weeks because she's meeting with students about their college essays. And I observed a teacher who was complaining of vertigo just moments before bending down to help a student pick up the contents of her spilled backpack.

According to the Center on the Social and Emotional Foundations for Early Learning (2005), you can convey warmth with facial expressions (especially smiling), laughing, a kind tone of voice, encouragement, or a special handshake. I protect my lunch time and feel too busy getting ready between classes to greet students at the door, but I remember and follow up with students about details about their lives, and I try my best to respond to student requests with a smile, patience, and kindness.

Amy Meredith, a sixth-grade language arts teacher at Community Middle School in Plainsboro, New Jersey, ends classes with a quick, warm, and encouraging exchange with her students. As students are packing up and leaving class, she smiles and calls out, "Don't just do well . . ." and the students finish the phrase in unison, "Do good!" She then responds in kind, "Go do some good out there!" Amy introduces this routine early in the year by reminding students that although we get focused on doing well in school and in life, it is essential that we find ways to do good deeds for others and "do good" in the world. She reinforces this concept throughout the year as class and schoolwide events offer her students opportunities to "do good" (A. Meredith, personal communication, December 3, 2019). We can all find ways to show warmth to students, but for those efforts to be effective, it must be honest and align with our own beliefs.

Partner With Parents

On back-to-school night, I try to spend the brief ten minutes I have with each group of parents mirroring the experience their children are having in my class with an emphasis on this balance between relationships and academics. Parents are automatically drawn to the pictures of their children around the room before finding a seat. I've come to realize these are the main questions parents want answered on back-to-school night.

- Is my child's teacher competent?
- What is the class's focus?
- How will the teacher grade my child's work?
- What kind of homework should my child expect?
- Will my child like this class?
- Is my child emotionally safe in this class?

I attempt to answer these questions with specific details as well as through my actions and the physical space of my classroom. In the short time we have together, I emphasize the importance of students at the high school level being advocates for themselves. I tell parents although I am, of course, receptive to their emails and concerns, they should encourage their children to talk to me themselves. I promise the parents I am a safe person to do this with, and I will never let their children down.

Questions for Reflection

Consider these questions after reading the chapter.

What specific behaviors, strategies, and activities am I currently doing in my classroom to build relationships with students?

____

____

Do I intentionally incorporate ways to get to know my students?

____

____

Do I repeatedly show students that they matter beyond their behavior or grade?

____

____

Do my words and actions demonstrate to students that I am someone they can rely on?

____

____

We need stories of belonging that move us towards each other, not from each other. This is what will save us. This is the work of peace. This is the work of imagination.

—Pádraig Ó Tuama

Moving Toward Belonging

Every subtle move teachers make—each poster we hang, each piece of student work decorating our walls, the way we greet students when they arrive, how we design activities, and even how we respond to students' questions—is intimately connected and works together to create a sense of belonging in the classroom. As teachers, we are the writers and narrators of this story; we are the architects of this design. All the specifications, measurements, and shadings are limited only by our imagination. If our design is structurally sound, it will support students as they engage in challenging work, ask questions, and listen to and implement critical feedback on their path to master the content and skills they will ultimately need for their lives beyond our classrooms.

Author Anne Lamott (2018a) writes that we should teach our children "they are preapproved. This is a come-as-you-are party. . . . It is okay for them to make bad mistakes and decisions" (p. 180). This chapter looks at the importance of students' connection to the class, themselves, others, and the work, and how teachers can foster this sense of belonging through their teaching practice and lesson design.

This chapter begins by examining belonging. You will find strategies and activities from my classroom as well as from other teachers across the grade levels for immediate use to help you devise ways to establish belonging—by helping students connect to the class, themselves, each other, and the work you do together.

Examining Belonging

Although students connect with one another during classes, lunchtime, club meetings, and athletic practices, there is a great deal of disconnection and loneliness in a typical classroom. Some students feel disconnected from one another as a result of social stigmas, insecurities, and misunderstandings. Other students are painfully shy, and peers with an incessant desire to be heard trample over them. Brown (2017), a vulnerability expert, writes, "Sometimes the most dangerous thing for kids is the silence that allows them to construct their own stories—stories that almost always cast them as alone and unworthy of love and belonging" (p. 15). And a classroom, even one with strong teacher and student relationships, isn't enough to establish belonging.

Brown (2017) defines belonging this way:

> Belonging is the innate human desire to be part of something larger than us. Because this yearning is so primal, we often try to acquire it by fitting in and by seeking approval, which are not only hollow substitutes for belonging, but often barriers to it . . . our sense of belonging can never be greater than our level of self-acceptance. (pp. 31–32)

Teachers see students desperately trying to fit in, joining clubs and activities in which they have no real interest, and allowing others to measure their self-worth in the form of grades, social media likes, casual remarks from peers, and whether they were selected for a particular team. Teachers need to be very concerned about students' social and emotional well-being because these struggles are inextricably linked to their academic performance: "Enhancing students' school belonging is of paramount importance for students' academic success and engagement, and must therefore be taken into account in educational programs, practice, and research" (St-Amand, Girard, & Smith, 2017, p. 115).

In one rehearsal, the middle school choir director burst into tears in the middle of the piece. She told us that she just felt so blessed to direct such a dedicated and talented group. Our singing made her feel the way she made us feel: special and important and loved. —Ninth grader

Brown (2017) makes the distinction that true belonging isn't being part of a team or in a group with a similar ideology, and just as in school, belonging shouldn't be contingent on a certain grade or particular expectation. True belonging is predicated on the premise that even if we show up as our messy, imperfect selves, we are still worthy. Teachers need to convey through words and lesson design that each student belongs in the class because his or her presence and contributions are essential to the learning experience. Plan ways for students to connect to the class, one another, themselves, and the work. Teachers' actions should resound these messages to students.

- You belong in this class because your presence is critical to the work we're doing.
- You belong in this class because your voice matters.
- You belong in this class because you matter.

According to a study on supporting social, emotional, and academic development:

> It is becoming clear that teachers and other school staff are in a unique position to change students' daily experiences and beliefs in ways that have real beneficial effects on students' academic performance.
>
> Four learning mindsets are particularly important in supporting students' academic behaviors, persistence, and performance on academic tasks. Expressed from the point of view of a student, the four mindsets are:
>
> - I belong in this learning community.
> - I can succeed at this.
> - My ability and competence grow with my effort (also known as a "growth mindset").
> - This work has value for me. (Allensworth et al., 2018, p. 13)

If teachers design learning experiences to nurture this sense of belonging, students feel more connected to the class, themselves, one another, and the work. A classroom with a sense of belonging is not a high-minded ideal disconnected from academics, high expectations, and improved learning outcomes. Instead, it is the solid foundation necessary for students to thrive.

As students struggle to figure out where they belong in the world, teachers have the power to improve learning outcomes by creating a place where they belong. Teachers can establish a sense of belonging for students by considering how to design classroom routines, expectations, and activities to foster connection and community. Teachers can also intentionally incorporate strategies and practices that further enhance students' sense of belonging. These components are critical, since "the ways that educators structure classes and build relationships with students influence students' feelings and perceptions about themselves, their class, the work, and school" (Allensworth et al., 2018, p. 6).

Establishing Belonging by Connecting With the Class

For students, school is life and life is school. When students arrive at a class where they feel like they can show up and be themselves, they are more likely to engage with one another and the work at hand: "Students with a sense of belonging and supportive relationships with teachers and classmates are more motivated to participate actively in the life of the classroom" (Mind Matters, n.d., p. 9).

My seventh-grade math teacher helped us learn in interesting ways, and he personally allowed me to be confident, to be weird or quirky, or whatever I wanted to be in the moment, which helped me become a bit more of who I really was—not just some quiet person doing their work. —Ninth grader

Consider routines, expectations, seating arrangements, personal demeanor, and even the classroom decor. Do not forget the teacher's enthusiasm and passion for school can infuse an excitement into class and the work (Patrick, Hisley, & Kempler, 2010). English teachers should be excited to join a student's book discussion, science teachers to roll up their sleeves and participate in lab experiments, and elementary teachers to sit cross-legged on the carpet to begin the morning meeting. If we don't love coming to school and believe in the value of the work we're doing, why should our students?

Connecting to the class can take lots of forms, and the following real-world scenarios provide numerous examples.

Brain Buzzers and Flashback Fridays

At Grover Middle School in West Windsor, New Jersey, eighth-grade mathematics teacher Zachary (Zak) Kumar welcomes his class each day by saying, "We're back and better than ever!" He calls his Do Now activity a brain buzzer and offers all students an opening activity with no right or wrong answers (Z. Kumar, personal communication, December 17, 2018). Some of his favorite questions include: What do you notice about . . .?, What's your preference about how to solve this problem?, and Which one do you think doesn't belong?

He is mindful not to check homework at the beginning of class, because he says, "It's not fun to start class with wrong answers."

In Zak's classroom, students can count on well-established routines and support systems. Students who were absent the prior day get their assignments from the Since You've Been Gone bin, and they can rely on starting their homework toward the end of class with visible answer sheets and teacher and peer support to minimize frustration levels at home. Zak carefully selects the types of problems, as well as how many problems students will practice at home because he says, "If you can do nine problems, you don't need to do eighteen." He labels the more difficult problems *challenge problems* to prepare students, and tells them in advance if a particular problem has a messy answer. Zak grades homework for attempted completion, not correctness.

Every Friday his class is Flashback Friday. He greets students with a song older than they are, which he uses as an entry point to review prior concepts and skills. This not only refreshes but also reinforces how much they've learned. He has a sign-up sheet for students to write down song requests for Flashback Friday, and they are, of course, thrilled if their song is chosen.

Zak's love of sports and Disney movies is apparent and provides an opening for students to ask him questions. They can always count on a game of trashketball, which Zak says, "offers kids the opportunity to be kids." During trashketball, students solve single mathematics problems on strips of paper. They bring their answers to him, and he initials the paper if the answer is correct. Then, students get to stand at the free-throw line (blue tape on the floor), crumple up the paper, and shoot it toward the garbage can. Students can earn homework passes and sometimes extra-credit points, but oftentimes they just do it for fun.

Classroom Playlist

In Taylor Sternotti's sixth-grade mathematics class at Community Middle School in Plainsboro, New Jersey, she creates a sense of inclusivity and belonging right at the beginning of the year by designing a student-generated playlist for each of her classes (T. Sternotti, personal communication, November 20, 2018). She sends out a Google Form asking students to select their theme song. Students listen to their class's unique playlist during their class time throughout the year. The playlist serves as a metaphor that honors her students' diverse voices and tastes. Their unique song selections open up conversations between Taylor and her students that further strengthen their relationship (figure 3.1, page 48).

Directions: Please write the name of one song that you feel defines who you are as a person, and tell me in one or two sentences how this song is a representation of you. The song must be appropriate for school, and I must be able to access it on Spotify.

Your first and last name: ______________________________

Class period: ______________________________

Song title and artist: ______________________________

I chose this song because ______________________________
______________________________.

Source: ©2019 by Taylor Sternotti. Used with permission.

Figure 3.1: If your life had a theme song, what would it be?

Visit **go.SolutionTree.com/literacy** for a free reproducible version of this figure.

Blogs and Identity Webs

Justin Dolcimascolo, a fourth- and fifth-grade technology teacher at Millstone River Elementary School in Plainsboro, New Jersey, strives to foster a sense of belonging in his class through a blogging platform (J. Dolcimascolo, personal communication, February 22, 2019). Students write about what they're passionate about, and other students comment. This activity seamlessly integrates all of the aspects of belonging—to yourself, the work, the class, and one another. Because his learning outcomes include digital citizenship, these activities lead students to learn how to treat one another online.

Justin strives to help students connect to themselves before trying to forge an authentic online connection among peers by beginning with an identity web, which he models for them with his own (figure 3.2).

Feminist writer and independent scholar Sara K. Ahmed (2018) inspired Justin's idea to have his students create their own identity webs. Ahmed (2018) explains:

> 'I am' statements . . . are a way for kids to reclaim their identity in case they have ever felt as if certain terms have been assigned to them. . . . When kids are empowered to announce to the world who they are, it is far less likely that someone else will do it for them. (p. 62)

Justin believes students can't bring their authentic selves into this online space without knowing who they are. He has learned through experience that students often identify themselves by external factors such as "I have a sister" or "I like sushi." He pushes students to understand themselves by challenging them to begin with *I am*

Source: Adapted from Ahmed, 2018. ©2019 by Justin Dolcimascolo. Used with permission.

Figure 3.2: Identity web teacher example.

statements. He will accept, "I am a sushi lover" because it usually comes with more authentic statements like "I am Muslim." Justin says, "Voice and choice don't mean anything if kids don't know who they are."

Once students identify who they are, Justin tasks them with honestly showing themselves to one another online, and he models and guides them on how to react and respond to one another. As this requires vulnerability and courage, Justin models the same for his students. Early in the year, when students ask him a question, he will clarify, "Just so you know, if you feel I'm not looking at you and listening, I am. I just have a lazy eye, and it sometimes wanders. I just want you to know that." When they talk about who is likely to get bullied in online spaces, and students chime in about weight and race, and a student says, "sexual orientation" to the confusion of some others, Justin will chime in with, "I'm gay, which is an example of sexual orientation. It means that I have a husband who is a man." In his teaching practice, Justin continually models openness and vulnerability for his students, and demonstrates that we can only truly belong to one another when we, in Ahmed's (2018) words, "announce to the world" who we are.

Similarly, when teachers welcome students to reveal who they are, we provide the opening to connect with one another by first connecting with themselves. In Brown's (2017) words, "True belonging only happens when we present our authentic, imperfect selves to the world" (p. 32). Justin is a prime example of how teachers are part of the design that makes all other parts work. Teachers are metaphorically one of the pillars in the classroom students rely on, much as they might a book or another indispensable resource. Student success is often predicated on their teacher's honesty, celebration of their uniqueness, and unwavering support.

Hattie's Seven Cs

Hattie (2012) writes:

> The picture of expert teachers . . . is one of involvement and respect for the students, of a willingness to be receptive to what the students need, of teachers who demonstrate a sense of responsibility in the learning process, and of teachers who are passionate about ensuring that their students are learning. (p. 27)

Hattie (2012) offers seven dimensions teachers should consider when evaluating how their current practices may be affecting their classroom climate. Figure 3.3 lists these dimensions, along with some questions teachers should use for self-assessment in each area.

Dimensions	Self-Assessment Questions
Care	In what specific ways do I demonstrate I care for students? In what specific ways do I try to understand how my students feel about things?
Control	In what observable ways do students treat me with respect? In what observable ways do the students and I make good use of our class time? In what observable ways do my students seem busy?
Clarify	What specific strategies do I use to clearly explain challenging topics?
Challenge	In what ways am I appropriately challenging my students? Do I differentiate based on readiness levels and offer open-ended opportunities for higher achievers? Do I offer opportunities for students to implement feedback and build their capacity to self-assess?

Captivate	In what ways do I attempt to make my lessons interesting? In what observable ways can I determine if students are interested? Do I offer students choices in process and product to increase levels of engagement? Do I vary my lessons in terms of activities, desk arrangement, and technology use?
Confer	In what observable ways do I provide opportunities for students to speak up and share their ideas about classwork? In what observable ways do I demonstrate respect for my students' ideas and suggestions?
Consolidate	How often do I use formative assessment to ascertain each student's level of understanding? In what specific ways do I offer students specific, actionable feedback?

Source: Adapted from Hattie, 2012.

Figure 3.3: The seven Cs of classroom climate—teacher self-assessment questions.

Another way teachers can use these seven dimensions to evaluate their classroom climate is by asking students to rate statements on a Likert scale, with, for example, 5 meaning they strongly agree and 1 meaning they strongly disagree (figure 3.4, page 52). This feedback is critical because according to Hattie (2012), students rate teachers higher on each dimension in classes with higher academic achievement gains. In addition, asking students for feedback on these seven Cs is a step toward improving classroom climate.

The teacher then analyzes students' perceptions of the class, and if he or she notices a pattern of low scores on one of the dimensions, the teacher asks more targeted follow-up questions to get more specific information. The teacher can then use this feedback to determine how to improve. Of course, like everything else, asking for feedback, analyzing the results, and following up with students are time consuming. In response, Wiggins (2012) reminds us, "Although the universal teacher lament that there's no time for such feedback is understandable, remember that 'no time to give and use feedback' actually means 'no time to cause learning.'" Wiggins's (2012) advice applies to both teachers and students.

Dimensions	Student Feedback Options
Care	*"My teacher . . . makes me feel that s/he really cares about me."* *"My teacher really tries to understand how students feel about things."*
Control	*"Students in this class treat the teacher with respect."* *"Our class stays busy and doesn't waste time."*
Clarify	*"My teacher has several good ways of explaining each topic that we cover in this class."* *"My teacher explains difficult things clearly."*
Challenge	*"In this class, we learn a lot almost every day."* *"In this class, we learn to correct our mistakes."*
Captivate	*"My teacher makes lessons interesting."* *"I like the ways in which we learn in this class."*
Confer	*"Students speak up and share their ideas about classwork."* *"My teacher respects my ideas and suggestions."*
Consolidate	*"My teacher checks to make sure that we understand when s/he is teaching us."* *"The comments that I get on my work in this class help me to understand how to improve."*

Source: Hattie, 2012, p. 31.

Figure 3.4: The seven Cs of classroom climate—student feedback.

Establishing Belonging by Connecting With Oneself

I try to impart to my students there is no one path to follow nor one road to success—and more than "two roads diverged in a yellow wood" (Frost, n.d.). The way to find meaning and purpose in life is to explore and pay attention to our own unique strengths, interests, passions, and curiosities. Although it may feel comforting to follow the steps on a well-worn path, we don't achieve fulfillment, or what Maslow (1943) calls self-actualization, by placing our feet neatly into the footsteps of another. For all of us, this reality is both liberating and frightening.

My highest aspiration for my students is for their confidence to grow as they acquire the knowledge and skills to help them become the best version of themselves. I want them to realize their own unique talents and abilities and be proud of what they have to offer. Poet Naomi Shihab Nye (n.d.) writes, "I want to be famous in the way a pulley is famous,/or a buttonhole, not because it did anything spectacular,/but because it never forgot what it could do." Students need to know there is no single measure for success, and their success may look different than everyone else's.

My Spanish teacher would ask us which toy to buy for his cat, which made us feel like our opinions mattered in more than just his class. He would joke around with those who showed effort in his class, implying that hard work doesn't have to be boring. He would always make pop culture references, making it apparent he knew what it was like to be a teenager, all the while helping us improve our Spanish. —Ninth grader

---

Ikigai

As teachers, we can select and utilize frameworks that help us align activities with our learning outcomes. We can then share these frameworks with our students, so they can apply them, think more deeply about themselves, integrate their identities and emerging senses of self into the work, and better understand the universe that is uniquely their own:

> As young people enter middle school and high school, they are often preoccupied with themselves and their peer groups. This is because an adolescent's primary "task," from a psychological standpoint, is to develop a healthy identity that can carry them into adulthood. . . . All of this comes into the classroom with them. To a large extent, how young people situate themselves in relation to academic learning will be shaped by the ways in which they see academic interest and competence as being aligned or misaligned with their developing social identities. (Allensworth et al., 2018, pp. 14–15)

We cannot separate our students' identities from our learning outcomes. Instead, we must integrate their social identities into the work we are doing together.

Early in the year, I introduce students to the Japanese concept of ikigai, or reason for being. I suggest that by finding the intersection of what you love, what you're good at, what the world needs, and maybe even what you can be paid for can help you narrow down your purpose and your path. I try to reinforce these concepts throughout the year to help students make personalized decisions when they are selecting topics for writing or research, choosing books to read, and making contributions in pairs, small groups, and whole-class discussions.

Happiness

There is much talk among students about a desire to be happy, and many students measure their happiness by external markers such as grades, awards, praise from adults, and acceptance from peers. I share psychiatrist Viktor Frankl's (1959/2007) quote with students:

> Don't aim at success. The more you aim at it and make it a target, the more you are going to miss it. For success, like happiness, cannot be pursued; it must ensue, and it only does so as the unintended side effect of one's personal dedication to a cause greater than oneself or as the by-product of one's surrender to a person other than oneself. Happiness must happen, and the same holds for success: you have to let it happen by not caring about it. (pp. 16–17)

Since this quote often confounds students at first, I further clarify Frankl's (1959/2007) meaning using the four pillars of happiness that author, speaker, and journalist Emily Esfahani Smith (2017) illustrates in her TED Talk, "There's More to Life Than Being Happy." I even have students chart an outline of each of the four pillars Smith (2017) discusses. For each pillar, I offer students reflective questions so they can identify how each pillar applies to their own lives. I try to remind students during the year to revisit and use these pillars to ground themselves when making decisions, and to infuse meaning into their lives when everything seems so overwhelming (figure 3.5).

Directions: Define the **Four Pillars of a Meaningful Life** for yourself.

Belonging: What are some of the relationships in which you feel valued for who you are? Think of your family and friends. *"Belonging comes from being in relationships where you're valued for who you are intrinsically and where you value others as well."*

Purpose: How do you use your strength to serve others? How do you contribute and feel needed? *"Without something worthwhile to do—people flounder."*

Transcendence: What activity gets you "in the zone" and helps you lose all sense of time and place? *"Transcendent states are those rare moments when you're lifted above the hustle and bustle of daily life, your sense of self fades away, and you feel connected to a higher reality."*

Storytelling: What story do you tell yourself about your life, your talents and abilities, and your future? *"Creating a narrative from the events of your life brings clarity. It helps you understand how you became you. But we don't always realize that we're the authors of our stories and can change the way we're telling them."*

Source: Adapted from Smith, 2017.

Figure 3.5: Finding your meaning and purpose questions.

Visit **go.SolutionTree.com/literacy** for a free reproducible version of this figure.

Metacognition Via Reflection

It is essential for teachers to build in opportunities for metacognition—for students to think about their own thinking. Students need time to reflect and think critically about the work they are doing in class so they can consider their strategies and approaches, time management, what worked and what didn't, why the content is important, and how it connects to their lives:

> Metacognition, simply put, is the process of thinking about thinking. . . . Perhaps the most important reason for developing metacognition is that it can improve the application of knowledge, skills, and character qualities in realms beyond the immediate context in which they were learned. (Fadel, Trilling, & Bialik, 2016)

Encouraging reflection also helps students consolidate their learning and aids in transfer—and in the process, helps students strengthen their understanding of themselves.

Offering students time to reflect echoes Brown's (2017) understanding of belonging: "Our sense of belonging can never be greater than our level of self-acceptance" (p. 32). In other words, if we don't give students time and space to understand themselves deeply, they will be unable to connect to each other, their peers, and the work everyone is doing together. Accepting ourselves is a precursor to our capacity to feel we belong in larger contexts. I generally rely on Jay McTighe's (2016) questions for reflection because teachers can easily adapt them for any type of reflection:

- What aspect of your work do you think was most effective? Why? How so?
- What aspect of your work do you think was least effective? Why? How so?

- What specific action(s) would improve your performance based on the feedback you received?
- What advice would you offer to next year's students to help their performance on this task?
- What did you learn from working on this task—about the content, topic, process, and/or yourself?

Listening to students' reflections can also help teachers create a sense of belonging in the classroom; an understanding of learners' needs helps them craft the space. Table 3.1 outlines students' developmental stages across grade levels, which can help teachers build a supportive classroom.

Table 3.1: Development Implications for Classroom Climate

Grade Band	Developmental Stage	Supportive Classroom Efforts
Grades 5–8	Concerned primarily with the self and their appearance and likeability, and identify themselves with their peer group	Ensure students feel respected and comfortable. Foster an inclusive classroom environment and provide psychological and physical safety for each student.
Grades 9–10	Actively developing their gender and cultural identity	Affirm students' social identities and connect these identities to intellectual growth and academic success. Offer texts presenting diverse voices of positive role models and a wide range of perspectives.
Grades 11–12	Focused on questions of meaning and purpose and where they belong in the world	Offer opportunities for students to make personal connections to their learning and apply their knowledge and skills to solving real-world problems.

Source: Adapted from Allensworth et al., 2018.

Establishing Belonging by Connecting With Others

According to psychologist Karyn Lewis (2016), "One way to foster connections is for teachers to actively work to find common ground with students and provide opportunities for students to recognize similarities among their peers." Students are in the process of forging their personal identities as they simultaneously strive to figure out how they fit into their peer group, and then what this all means for them academically. Teachers can use this time of curiosity and identity seeking to create learning opportunities that foster collaboration and teamwork to help students build relationships with one another. These experiences also have the capacity to lead students to further success both academically and behaviorally in the classroom and beyond. Lewis (2016) further clarifies this point:

> Belonging acts as a precursor to other aspects of positive functioning in the classroom. For instance, when students feel like they belong, they show more motivation, engagement, and self-efficacy. Thus, social belonging is one of the first things educators should attend to because when it's lacking, students find it difficult to succeed academically and are less likely to thrive.

I play the violin, but I am so insecure about my playing because of a minor disability. I explained to the teacher what I could do and couldn't do. This teacher smiled and said one thing that I still remember to this day: "It doesn't matter as long as you love to play." It gave me confidence in my own playing. —Ninth grader

---

Mutual Support

At the beginning of the school year, students and I were talking in class about abridged and unabridged versions of class novels when one student raised his hand and asked, "What does unabridged mean?" I snapped my fingers and thanked him for being brave enough to ask the question. It had not occurred to me to define these terms, and this moment reminded me of my expert blind spot, which Wiggins and McTighe (2005) describe so eloquently: "What is obvious to us is rarely obvious to a novice—and was once not obvious to us either, but we have forgotten our former views and struggles" (p. 138). We cannot, of course, always account for our blind spots, but we can encourage students to support one another when our expertise gets in the way.

During one presentation, a student struggled to get the words out; we all patiently waited. His voice was trembling, and he repeatedly inhaled deeply to calm himself. I sat in the back of the room frantically wondering how long to let this go on or if he was going to pull himself together, and what I could possibly do in the moment to help him. In the midst of my internal debate, I began to hear quiet snaps in the classroom. Brown (2010) writes, "Connection is the energy between people when they feel seen, heard, and valued" (p. 19). The energy in the room, and others' audible support, gave him the courage to continue. This is belonging.

Collaborative Peer-to-Peer Learning

Teachers also support students by offering them opportunities to connect with one another through collaborative learning activities. Students work in various groupings (across skill levels and personality types) throughout the school year, and I do (albeit infrequently) let students work with their friends. My students understand that, often, working with friends is not the most productive arrangement, but the occasional opportunity to decide whom they work with is crucial to fostering a sense of belonging.

Regardless of the student groupings, it is essential teacher-designed collaborative activities are group worthy (Lotan, 2003) and foster connection. Teachers can achieve this by requiring students to contribute their perspectives and individual strengths with the overall goal of creating something new together. Table 3.2 provides the design features of group-worthy tasks, along with a description and examples of each feature.

Table 3.2: Group-Worthy Tasks

Design Feature	Description	Examples
Remains "open-ended and require[s] complex problem solving" (p. 72)	Offers problems (authentic, if possible) that have multiple solutions with different pathways for solving Requires analysis, interpretation, synthesis, evaluation, and justification	• Conducting experiments • Building models • Analyzing literary passages • Solving mathematical problems or real-world issues

Includes "multiple entry points to the task and multiple opportunities to show intellectual competence" (p. 72)	Allows students to use their unique talents and abilities to collaboratively problem solve	• Gathering data by doing the following
		  ○ Listening to an audiobook or podcast
		  ○ Interpreting a chart or an infographic
		  ○ Researching in a book or online database
		• Demonstrating understanding by doing the following
		  ○ Creating a graphic design
		  ○ Building models
		  ○ Writing text
		  ○ Handling the presentation's speaking portions

Focuses on "discipline-based, intellectually important content" (p. 72)	Aligns to the standards, curriculum, essential questions, and enduring understandings	• All activities align with the curriculum, involve complex tasks that require problem solving, and, when possible, connect to real-world issues.
Requires "positive interdependence as well as individual accountability" (p. 72)	Requires each group member to play a significant role that is measurable and contributes meaningfully to the whole during the process, as well as in the final product	• Contributions from each student that inspire and elevate other students (such as the graphic designer's work in a social media campaign possibly sparking new insight into the writer's copy) • Assessment that applies to the group overall as well as to individual contributions
Includes "clear criteria for the evaluation of the group's product" (p. 72)	Requires giving criteria to students prior to beginning the task and giving actionable feedback during the process	• Students co-creating rubrics under the teacher's guidance using exemplars (real world if possible) to determine a product's qualities

Source: Adapted from Lotan, 2003.

Another important consideration when designing collaborative peer-to-peer learning activities is time. I try to give students enough time in class to work together. Even though technology easily allows students to work together beyond the school day, it presumes there are equitable resources and there is often uneven participation outside school. The workload then inevitably falls on one or two students, and this breaks down relationships instead of fostering the connections teachers are trying so hard to build. Furthermore, teachers need to be mindful about how we assess group activities, as this can build resentment among students if some feel other students are unfairly rewarded as a result of their hard work. My easy solution is any overall group grade that is generally low stakes and, since the tasks are group-worthy, assessing students primarily on their individual accountability.

Seeing the Connection

Teachers can foster a sense of belonging within current classwork by building in opportunities for students to recognize that we all are inextricably connected and have more in common than we realize. We can do this through reading stories that explore universal themes in English class, making connections in history between the past and modern day, learning about biology and genetics in science, and offering students the opportunity to have guided and purposeful, yet self-directed, conversations. Ask yourself questions like the following.

- "How can my classroom contain a visual representation of all of my students in a way that celebrates our similarities and differences?"
- "In what ways can students access another's thinking to recognize and understand varying perspectives?"
- "How can students work together with other students to inform and elevate their own work?"
- "Is there a way for students to use other students' final products to create something entirely new and representative of *all* learners in class?"

Poet Mary Oliver (2016) writes about Edgar Allan Poe's "artistically kaleidoscopic brilliance" in which he "does not write only about his own argument with the universe, but about everyone's argument" (p. 90). Oliver's (2016) words remind me of the beauty, wonder, and universality of our experiences.

As our students enter middle school, the shift from one teacher to multiple teachers changes their sense of connectivity to their classmates. My students have remarked to me that in some classes, they don't even know everyone's names. Rebecca King's fourth-grade classroom can inspire secondary teachers to create this sense of belonging to one another for older students with her display of finger-painted student names:

> The kids fingerprint and blend their color with another to make a new color where they overlap. They also write their names in their spots. The kids then write how they plan on mixing well together this year or how they hope to mix well with classmates and community this year. (R. King, personal communication, November 14, 2018)

There is a twelfth-grade classroom in my district decorated with student poems modeled after George Ella Lyon's (1999) "Where I'm From" poem. Lyon's (1999) poem (https://bit.ly/2bSJWP6) provides a clear model from which students can mimic her allusions and metaphors as they explore their own identities and truths. These seniors also added personal pictures to their display to further illustrate where they are from. To help them recognize the connections between themselves and their classmates, teachers can guide students with questions such as the following.

- "How are we all 'from' artifacts, moments, families, hopes, and dreams?"
- "Whose poem reveals details that seem much different from how you might have perceived them?"
- "If you see threads between your classmates' poems, what do you think this says about the universal human experience?"
- "What have you learned from this exercise?"

Hearing the Connection

My favorite project to build a sense of connectedness and belonging is an assignment that begins with students emulating Hughes's (2001) "Theme for English B" and culminates in the Echoes Project, when they share their poems with the class, and pull lines they choose from each other's work into a single poem. I tell students one way we find empathy for and build connection with one another is by sharing personal details about ourselves. I explain from an outside perspective, we all seem so different, yet when we offer a glimpse of our personal struggles and some insight into who we are, we see that we are more the same than we are different and feel less alone. I remind students to be open and honest, but only to the extent they feel comfortable. I model my own poem, and students perform these spoken word poems. Figure 3.6 details how teachers can inspire students to compose their own poem.

As students begin crafting their poems in class, many are unsure about what personal details might be OK to share. For this assignment and many others, I encourage students to get out of their comfort zone, and I draw the image shown in figure 3.7 (page 62) through the year to remind them that in order to learn and grow, you sometimes need to be a little uncomfortable. I'll ask them how they can get out of their comfort zone, yet stay in their growth zone. I also ask, "What is your plus-one?" Our plus-one is pushing ourselves just a little further than we normally would, taking a small risk, or going one step beyond what we've done before. I enthusiastically and often write "What is your plus-one?" on the board, and I model my plus-one for students.

Guiding questions: How does learning about others lead us to empathize with them? How does learning about others help us to be more compassionate toward ourselves? How does understanding other people's perspectives enable us to be grateful for the gifts in our own life as well as make us happier?

Your task: After reading and discussing Hughes's (2001) "Theme for English B," you now have the same directions Hughes had. Write a thirty- to forty-line poem that only you could have written. *You may either recite your poem or create a video we will watch together in class.*

Your purpose: Create a spoken word poem in which you share specific details about yourself others may not know. Your poem should show that although in many ways you are unique, you are also the same as the rest of us. Your goal is to make the listener feel like he or she knows you on a more personal level—to make the listener feel connected to you. Let's see how we are more the same than we are different.

The audience: Your teacher and your peers

Continued ▶

Figure 3.6: "Theme for English B" spoken word poetry.

Stanza one: Simply copy Hughes's first stanza and include it in your poem.

Stanza two: Your first line should start something like Hughes's: "I wonder if it's that simple?"

Then, write between ten and fifteen lines about who you are and where you're from. You might want to include these details.

- Age
- Race or religion
- Hometown or neighborhood
- Family life

Stanza three: Write between twenty and twenty-five lines about who you are, what you are like, what matters to you, and how you see yourself. Try to include the following.

- Your first line should start something like Hughes's: "It's not easy to know what is true for you or me . . . "
- Your likes and dislikes
- Your beliefs, morals, values, or any motto you live by
- Physical characteristics, ethnicity, religion, or family traditions
- Favorite memories or important relationships
- Maybe even finish the stanza with your initial thoughts of me (the teacher), this class, or this school.

Stanza four: Simply finish off your poem with Hughes's following line:

"This is my page for English B."

Source: Adapted from Hughes, 2001.

Visit **go.SolutionTree.com/literacy** for a free reproducible version of this figure.

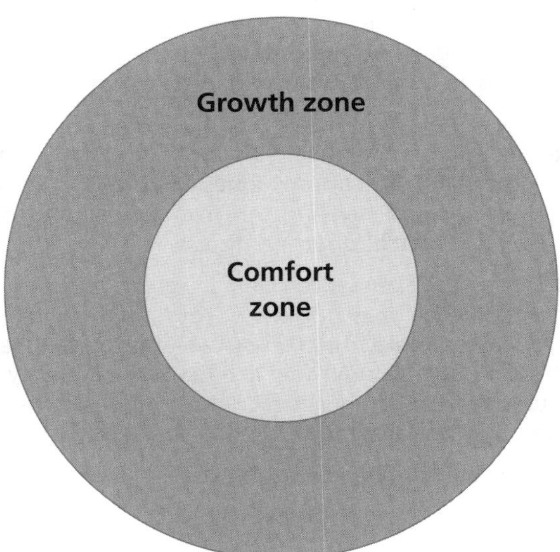

Figure 3.7: Comfort zone and growth zone.

This framework prompts students to consider sharing more personal opinions—those that are revealing and often vulnerable and honest. If students don't reveal themselves, they are not opening themselves to connection. If we give students time to reflect on these kinds of questions, they can learn things about themselves and others.

After this kind of prompting, one student asked if it was OK to say she hates going to church; another student asked if it was OK to say people always ask if she can see out of her eyes because they are so slanted; and another asked if it was OK to write that people ask how someone can be Christian if they're not white. Their honesty and willingness to be vulnerable were staggering, and beyond what I had even hoped for. As these voices echoed in my head (they all felt so similar and yet so different), I thought, "We need to do something with these lines." After students performed their spoken word poems, I had them compile their favorite lines from others' poems to create a new product, which we named the Echoes Project (figure 3.8).

> I'm not sure what I want to be. I'm not even sure who I want to be.
>
> I'm a Christian, but only pray when I want something.
>
> Too old to scream and cry, but too young to work full time.
>
> We all have different pages colored with different colors and erased with different erasers.
>
> We grew up with each other, so I guess a part of you is embedded in me and a little part of me is embedded in you.

Source: ©2019 by Sruti Bapatla, Justin Gong, Madeline Holmes, Katherine Lu, & Myka Melville. Used with permission.

Figure 3.8: "Theme for English B" lines from student poems for the Echoes Project.

Students created found poems, songs, videos, and dances, and even a music video that included students who weren't even in the class! There was a daily desk calendar, featuring a garland with quotes hanging from it and brilliant artwork. Students were honored and humbled to see their peers create artwork out of their words; our classroom, which we later decorated with these Echoes Projects, became an implicit reminder of our connection to each other. As Wormeli (2016) states, "students' learning is markedly influenced by their connectedness with the adults in charge, classmates, and the larger community." More than any other project, the Echoes Project forges connections and builds community, and it strengthens many students' resolve to take even further academic risks.

Establishing Belonging by Connecting to the Work

According to a study on social, emotional, and academic development:

> Students learn by actively working with material, and it is that process of grappling that allows new skills and content to stick (Bransford, Brown, & Cocking, 1999). . . . The degree to which students feel interested and connected is consequential to their learning and future engagement. . . . The more students are emotionally engaged in school, the more easily they can focus their attention and direct their behavior toward learning (Mahatmya, Lohman, Matjasko, & Farb, 2018; Steele, 1997). (Allensworth et al., 2018, p. 3)

It makes sense that to fully create a sense of belonging in our classrooms, we need to design activities to help our students feel connected to the work we're doing. Students, like adults, experience higher engagement when they are curious and interested in the work they are doing. For example, if you are planning a trip that you've waited years to take, you might carefully research the area, map out places to visit, plan out your time, and read and ask questions about the destination. Joseph Campbell (as cited in Brown, 2012, p. 40) writes, "If you can see your path laid out in front of you stop by stop, you know it's not your path. Your own path you make with every step you take. That's why it's your path."

As much as possible, students need the freedom to forge their own paths so they can actively engage in the work you are doing together. You can see how belonging and learning go hand in hand:

> Powerful learning—not only in school, but also in life—occurs when learners are trying to produce or do something consequential, when they see the purpose in what they are doing, when they have some choice about what they learn, when they are receiving regular feedback on their work, and when they are part of a community that supports them but also holds them to high standards. (Mehta & Fine, 2019)

My third-grade teacher's motto was "I'd rather you make a mistake than get it right." This just made me a lot more comfortable asking questions, and in turn it helped me take more risks when doing work, like trying a problem without asking for help or looking at the answer key. —Ninth grader

---

Relevance

Teachers should ensure all activities are accessible to students regardless of their academic, physical, and social-emotional skill levels. The level of difficulty will always ultimately reflect their grade level, but all students must have an entry point to begin. For some students, teachers may need to scaffold the early stages, whereas others may be more independent. If the work is immediately too difficult for students, they can't possibly connect to the work.

We can then foster our students' connection to the work we're doing by explaining to them why the work matters beyond the classroom. According to Pink (as cited in Azzam, 2014):

> Responding to the "why" question is especially important for kids. When kids ask, "Why are we doing this?" we often dismiss it as an annoying question when, in fact, it's a pretty darn good one. And we need to be able to answer it—not to placate the kids, but because there's a rich body of evidence showing that when people know why they're doing something, they do it better.

Another way to help students connect to the work is to move beyond explaining the why and offering them learning opportunities with meaning and purpose that have a clear connection to their lives beyond school. Students should be able to see themselves in what we read together in school, and understand how the work we're doing is relevant to their lives. Students should have choices with these activities, where they are exploring a problem they want to solve, contemplating questions they are curious to answer, and doing work they care about. As Wormeli (2016) writes, "Teaching is done with students, not to them."

My fourth-grade teacher helped me a lot! When she gave me and my classmates a challenge, she expected everybody to finish it, even if it was really hard. She expected us to not give up. From her I learned that even if you are doing the hardest thing you've ever done in your life, you shouldn't give up on it because in everything you do, you learn something new. —Fifth grader

---

It is therefore the job of teachers to scaffold the work, create space for students to engage in the work, and provide support along the way. One way to get everyone settled but busy with something relevant while waiting for class to start is with a Do Now. The Do Now activity is generally a quick one students can begin independently as soon as they enter the classroom. The hallmarks of a Do Now are equity and engagement accessible to all students and that pique their interest, igniting engagement. It is also a great way to transition from one subject to the next, because it can provide a pathway to activate the schema required to connect new learning to prior knowledge. Teachers across grade levels and content areas can use Do Now to reinforce previously taught concepts through puzzles, riddles, games, word sorts, manipulatives, or open-ended questions—whatever is most likely to capture students' interest, extend their thinking, and serve as an entry point to the new content. Since the Do Now activity guarantees each student a successful outcome, it fuels connection to the work.

I call our Do Now activities Quotes of the Week. I created a presentation to use throughout the entire school year, and the objective is for students to settle into class, connect briefly with one another, and self-reflect. We spend two days on each quote and generally less than five minutes on any given day. On our first day, I display the quote on a SMART Board for students to copy down while I read it aloud. This routine takes only the first few minutes of class while students unpack and settle in. On the second day, I display the same quote, read it aloud, and pose some questions designed to help students interpret the quote's meaning. Depending on the level of difficulty, I approach the interpretation in different ways.

- If I think it's easy to interpret, students write first and, when the keyboard clicks quiet, a few students share their ideas in small groups (and then sometimes with the whole class).
- If I think the quote is challenging, I pose targeted questions, students talk in their groups, and then I ask them to share their interpretations until we reach multiple meanings. Students then have time to write down their personal reflections.

I circulate during the Do Now activity to ensure students are on task, and I check their documents for completion once per marking period. I've had students complete the Do Now activity in their composition notebooks and Google Classroom. Visit **go.SolutionTree.com/literacy** for a free reproducible version of the form.

Basic Needs

Figure 3.9 depicts the basic needs we all require to thrive (Maslow, 1943). Once scaffolding is in place, contemplate ways to design lessons and activities to honor and recognize the individuality of all learners as we support them on their path to reach their full potential.

I've thought for a long time about exactly what it means to meet our students' basic needs and how, in so many ways, they are very much the same as we are. I've come to understand it as this:

> Like adults, students feel valued and respected when an experience challenges them, reflects their interests, and allows

> their voices to be heard. And when they are the authors of their own stories, they attend to each moment because they care deeply about the rising action, the falling action, and the resolution—the triumphs and the lessons are their own. (Pandolpho, 2018c)

When students feel connected to teachers and have a sense of belonging, teachers can be the helpers and mentors who help students as they become the hero of their own journeys.

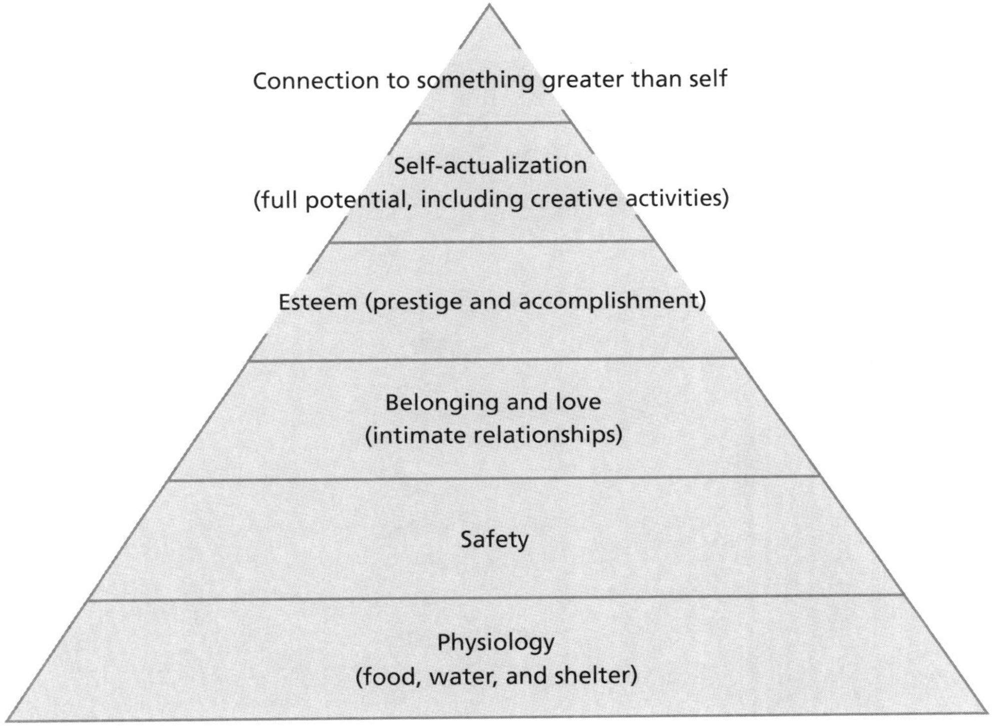

Source: Adapted from Maslow, 1943.

Figure 3.9: Maslow's (1943) hierarchy of needs.

Questions for Reflection

Consider these questions after reading the chapter.

In what ways can I foster a sense of belonging with a visual representation of the learners in my classroom?

____

____

In what ways can I build a sense of belonging in my classroom through daily routines and expectations?

How can I further use the ideas in this chapter as inspiration to help my students do the following?

- Connect to our class
- Connect with themselves
- Connect with one another
- Connect to the work we do together

Part II

Supporting the Development of Literacy Skills Built on the Foundation of Relationships and Belonging

That is the part of the beauty of all literature. You discover that your longings are universal longings, that you're not lonely and isolated from anyone. You belong.

—F. Scott Fitzgerald

Developing Readers

Many of my students consider themselves writers, but they are reluctant readers. I remind them that reading will make them better writers, as reading fills us with words and ideas, so when we write, the words pour out powerfully and eloquently onto the page. Yet, there are many other reasons it is essential to cultivate a life of reading: books somehow manage to express precisely what we feel, but have never been quite able to articulate, and help us realize a thought or an impulse we've long been ashamed of is exactly the same as a character we've come to love and admire. They help us feel like we belong. Books can comfort us when we're feeling lonely, disconnected, or afraid, and can energize us as they unravel the mysteries of life and illuminate concepts we had been unable to grasp before. Reading helps us better understand ourselves and the world around us and can fortify us with the grit and resilience we need to withstand life's inherent difficulties. Further, neuroscientist Julianne Chiaet (2013) discovered that "literary fiction improves a reader's capacity to understand what others are thinking and feeling," which builds empathy and strengthens our capacity to embrace the understanding that we truly belong to one another.

As readers, we derive strength from learning how to resolve conflicts and confront hardship, with the understanding that we can emerge stronger as a result. These are not small things.

I remind my students we have infinite space inside us to grow and change, and there are endless possibilities for what we can do or become. Yet, it is up to us to take advantage of the means available, and books are one of our most precious resources. Reading is the great unifier of all of the disciplines; students who are proficient readers perform better in every subject. Author and former administrator, teacher, and coach Mike Schmoker (2006) writes in *Results Now*, "The lifelong consequences of good—or poor—literacy skills are monumental. . . . they affect not only school success, but intelligence itself—our ability to think" (p. 52). When we read, the world outstretches before us as the text leads us to information we never imagined and questions we never thought to ask. We marvel when we learn that a historical event mirrors what is happening in modern-day politics, when we discover the scientific theory that explains how ice is actually less dense than water, and when we realize that our pursuit for success and happiness should really be a search for meaning.

The benefits of developing strong reading skills are without question. According to the National Endowment for the Arts's (2007) research report *To Read or Not to Read*, "Greater academic, professional, and civic benefits [are] associated with high levels of leisure reading and reading comprehension" (p. 94). Reading also has benefits that extend beyond the immediate meaning derived from particular texts. Professor emeritus at the University of Southern California Stephen D. Krashen (2004) writes, "There is little doubt that reading influences cognitive development . . . Good thinkers . . . read a great deal and have read a great deal" (pp. 35–36).

In this chapter, we'll look at how we can plan backward to answer the question, Who do we want our students to be as readers? To me, the answer is, we want them to become independent, fluent readers across a variety of materials and texts so they can become critical thinkers and informed citizens. We want our students to appreciate the power of words and the impact of writing style, and understand the universality of the human experience—and in the process, feel more connected to one another. To develop students as readers, teachers need to create learning experiences that allow students to grapple with primary source documents, read fiction and nonfiction texts, glean the wisdom of the ages, and rejoice in the shared experience of stories.

This chapter includes ideas and strategies for immediate use with the potential to help students achieve these learning outcomes and, along the way, continue to strengthen relationships and fortify their sense of belonging. Teachers can apply these strategies across grades levels and disciplines with the underlying goals of teaching students to read for understanding through the thoughtful exploration of the complexity of people and our world as they begin to recognize their needs and habits as readers.

Reading in a Learner-Centered Classroom

In *The Book Whisperer*, author and teacher Donalyn Miller (2009) writes:

> The fact that educators have coined the terms *real reading*, *authentic reading*, and *independent reading* to differentiate what readers do in school from what readers do in life is part of the problem. Why does it have to be different? Why is the goal of reading instruction disconnected from reading in the rest of a student's life? (p. 4)

The answer is, it doesn't have to be.

In a learner-centered classroom, texts mirror the real world and instruction supports students as readers beyond the classroom. Teachers offer strategies through the reading and analysis of challenging texts to help students hone their reading skills and build cultural literacy in the process. We listen to our students talk or write about books they're excited about, and offer them feedback to help them advance as readers. We model literacy and share with students what we read, how we find time to read, and how we continue learning through reading. Of course, teachers must ensure all learning opportunities align with objectives, standards, and the curriculum, as they simultaneously invite students to the table so their voices can be heard.

I remember that our kindergarten teacher said, "Imagine you're a super reader! All of the words you read, you understand. Reading is your superpower!" This may sound silly, but to me, a five-year-old, it changed my world. Imagining this gave me patience to practice reading and to read more often. —Ninth grader

---

When students read in my class, some students listen to an audiobook and follow along with the text, some prefer to read in complete silence, and others read while listening to music. When my students annotate, some students use a complex color-coding system of sticky notes, but others are minimalists. Choice while reading communicates to students that I accept them for who they are and honor and respect their preferences; this can lead to students perceiving "classroom activities as more important" (Marzano Resources, n.d.). The shared experiences of whole-class texts and choice books lead teachers to personal and thoughtful conversations with students that have the power to build and strengthen relationships. Here is how to begin.

To Begin

According to Wiggins (2015), "the main purposes for reading are gaining meaning and gaining knowledge." However, with the best intentions, teachers may cloud this purpose by inundating students with reading logs, vocabulary words, questions, and stringent note-taking guidelines. Although these may be worthwhile endeavors, to students it may seem that teachers have created a complicated and disconnected mess of the essence of reading. Schmoker (2006) writes, "Our preoccupation with basic literacy, with decoding and fluency, may be preventing us from helping students to acquire the most important and practical forms of reading—where we read for meaning" (p. 58).

It might seem overly simplistic to remind students the main purpose of reading is to construct meaning, and yet it is always beneficial to share with students why we are doing what we are doing:

> Two powerful ways of increasing impact are to know *and* share both the learning intentions and success criteria of the lesson with students. When students know both, they are more likely to work towards mastering the criteria of success, more likely to know where they are on the trajectory towards this success, and more likely to have a good chance of learning how to monitor and self-regulate their progress. (Hattie, 2012, p. 67)

If teachers begin by telling students the main purpose for reading is to find meaning and gain knowledge, they immediately understand all other tasks are in the service of accomplishing these goals.

Wiggins (2015) recommends teachers introduce two or three strategies students may need to construct meaning for a lesson focused on meaning making. He describes reading strategies as "tools for understanding the conceptual content of text" (Wiggins, 2015). As teachers, we gradually fill this toolbox and foster our students' ability to decide which tool they need to use when. We offer strategies: "Here's how you annotate," "Here are some effective ways to use sticky notes," or "Here are some ways to analyze different aspects of a text." Then, as students begin to understand their needs as readers, we offer them metacognitive time to reflect on their process, decide what works for them, and then explicitly teach them how to transfer these skills to their reading lives beyond our classroom.

In third grade, I was placed in a special program because I was reading below grade level. I felt ashamed that my reading skills were low. But this special teacher was encouraging, kind, and had a soothing voice. Reading beside this special teacher was so comforting to me, it made me love to read. —Ninth grader

---

Teachers should pair a firmly established choice reading program with the thoughtful analyses of challenging whole-class texts to provide students with balanced and substantive reading instruction. We need to avoid a "forced march through books," and Wiggins (as cited in Sztabnik, n.d.) suggests teachers ask themselves these questions.

- "What are you going to do to cause a difference in students based on that book?"
- "What are you going to do that is going to cause a change in the learner?"

With these guiding questions, teachers should teach strategies students can easily adapt for whole-class texts, book clubs, or independent reading. Teachers can model the reading process of making predictions, asking questions, rereading difficult sections, and giving students time to practice these strategies. Teachers can help students access the minds and hearts of fully realized characters to understand different perspectives, the conflicts inherent in life, and how to seek resolutions. High school English language arts teacher and author Kelly Gallagher (2009) writes, "Teachers have a duty to challenge students with complex novels and longer works" (p. 57), adding, "It's not just a story; it's an imaginative rehearsal for living a productive life as an adult" (p. 79).

A whole-class text in the hands of a skilled teacher can impart this gift to students—a gift they desperately need. Teachers can apply the activities in this chapter to whole-class texts, as well as when students are reading books of their own choosing.

Reading Activities

Reading is a complex process and students may be reading different texts, so there is no formula or procedure for understanding a text. Therefore, teachers must offer students a comprehensive plan with many options, so they can increasingly become more proficient, independent readers. Providing students with this sense of autonomy reaffirms their sense of belonging in your classroom. You are communicating to students that everyone is there to become more proficient readers and critical thinkers, and that you are there to offer tools that will help them reach that end in a way that is uniquely their own. Consider the following reading activities.

My second-grade teacher told me that I could read well if I set my mind to it. She inspired me to read to the point where I would stay up late to read a book. By that December, I became the best reader in my class. —Ninth grader

---

Iceberg Approach

Kaitlyn (Kaity) Haley, an eighth-grade history teacher at Grover Middle School in West Windsor, New Jersey, offers her students a personalized approach to understanding text (K. Haley, personal communication, June 10, 2019). As she teaches students at different reading levels, Kaity gives students varying entry points to a text. She uses an iceberg graphic (figure 4.1) because the metaphor is nonjudgmental, and it gives students language to understand themselves as readers. If students are asking and answering who, what, where, and when questions as they read, they can identify themselves as reading at the surface level. If they are asking and answering why and how questions, they can identify themselves as reading at a deeper level. Since students apply the iceberg method to different texts, they will notice that the level varies depending on the particular reading. Kaity says the iceberg reading method helps "you learn about who you are, and it unites all of us" (K. Haley, personal communication, June 10, 2019). Students can all be on different parts of the iceberg at different times, but they are all on the iceberg together.

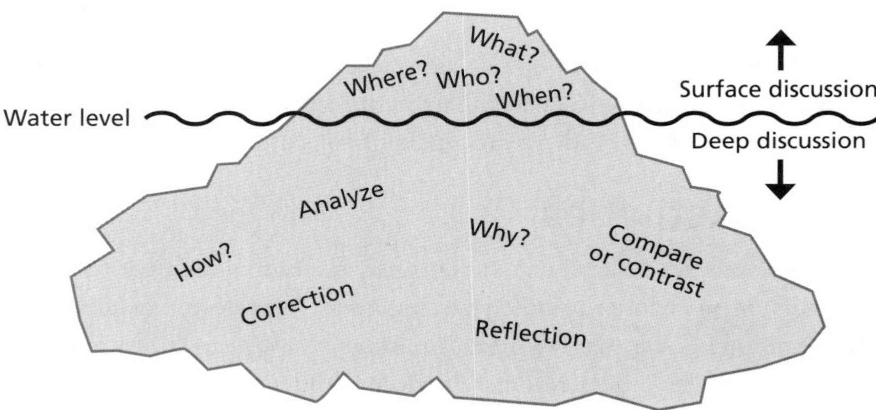

Source: ©2019 by Kaitlyn Haley. Used with permission.

Figure 4.1: Iceberg approach to reading.

Visit **go.SolutionTree.com/literacy** for a free reproducible version of this figure.

Students at a more basic comprehension level quickly realize they must begin at the surface level of the text, whereas more advanced readers immediately go deeper to more independently analyze the text and consider higher-level questions.

When her eighth graders learn about various world religions, Kaity offers them readings that support these varying entry points, often with charts and graphs accessible to students with differing reading levels. The following, from Pew Research Center (2017), is one such example:

> In total, nearly half of Muslims (48%) say they have experienced at least one of these types of discrimination over the past year, which is up slightly from 2011 (43%) and 2007 (40%). In addition, nearly one-in-five U.S. Muslims (18%) say they have seen anti-Muslim graffiti in their local community in the last 12 months.
>
> "I have definitely experienced both [discrimination and support]. I've had people make comments and of course they'll give me weird looks and things like that. But I've definitely heard people [make] rude comments straight to my face. I've also had people say really nice things about my hijab, or say it's beautiful or say they think my religion is beautiful." —Muslim woman under 30
>
> "I have a lot of friends, and just community members, who are very open—who are glad to have this kind of diversity in their community, where there aren't a lot of Muslims at all. I'm probably the only Muslim they know or they'll ever know. And they're glad for that, and they like to give support and be there." —Muslim man under 30

You can find diverse texts at these sites as well.

- Kelly Gallagher's Building Deeper Readers & Writers (www.kellygallagher.org/article-of-the-week)
- Newsela (https://newsela.com)
- Teaching Tolerance (www.tolerance.org/classroom-resources/texts)

Kaity's inclusive approach to honoring her students as readers parallels the way she teaches her students to view other people's differences. This approach supports the students' sense of belonging in her classroom; Kaity's students know she accepts them for exactly who they are. This strategic approach to texts meets many common state standards because it supports students as they read and comprehend grade-level texts of varying levels of complexity.

Giving Access to Your Thinking With a Think-Aloud

Once students identify their approach to a text, teachers can offer minilessons on reading strategies throughout the year. When I introduce a reading strategy, I often use the think-aloud. I make my thinking visible by walking students through each step using a SMART Board or document camera, so students can listen to what I'm thinking, understand that I sometimes have to make more than one attempt before I get it right, and see how the strategy unfolds and leads to a final product.

When teachers offer this type of clarity and accessibility, they not only scaffold an activity for students but also offer insight into their own thinking, demonstrating how they go through the same complex processes students do to reach a conclusion. This strategy further builds a sense of belonging, because it communicates to students, "You are not alone. I go through the same struggles you do." It enables students to feel closer to you as you invite them to watch you try, fail, and try again. Modeling ourselves as thinkers and learners can also help students become more self-reflective about their own complex processes. These types of lessons should be purposefully brief to have the desired impact because (truthfully) watching a teacher model a reading strategy can quickly devolve into drudgery.

Annotating

At the beginning of the school year, annotation strategies are one of the first techniques I model and think aloud for students, because they reflect a skill referenced in many state standards. Annotating helps students construct implicit and explicit meaning, notice authors' craft moves, and determine how word choice affects overall meaning and tone, which are skills referenced in many state standards. I tell students they ultimately must figure out an annotating method that feels comfortable to them because this is a skill they will need in school and beyond. I support this idea by reminding students during the year they need to annotate to the extent it works for them. Therefore, although I do often require students to annotate, I do not insist they abide by very specific guidelines. I want to honor their individuality and give them the autonomy to make these choices on their own because I believe in their ability to do so. Schmoker (2006) writes:

> Close, strategic reading is one of the most powerful and enjoyable ways to develop the ability to think critically and evaluate information—to literally *become smart.* (p. 59)
>
> Close, critical, strategic reading—with pen in hand—needs to occupy a substantial portion of every school day. (p. 61)

In order for annotation to become a lifelong habit, students must decide on an annotation system that works for them.

I teach annotation strategies by projecting a document on a SMART Board with a highlighter and a pen in hand. I explain to students to consider each paragraph a unit of thought, and that a helpful guideline is to highlight only one main idea per paragraph and make one annotation. I generally model how to annotate using the first two paragraphs of the text. I read the paragraph aloud, tell them what I'm thinking, and then explain how I choose what to highlight. Then, I rephrase the main ideas in each paragraph to show them how they should write notes in the margin in their own words, perhaps with abbreviations and symbols. I suggest using pencil so they can easily erase their notes (Zucker, 2016). I explain that marginal notes are where we demonstrate our understanding to our future selves when we review the chapter, and that if we annotate well, it ensures that we won't ever have to reread the chapter. Thus, by annotating, we are creating kind of a cheat sheet for ourselves.

For these first two paragraphs, students copy my model annotations to use as an example, and I encourage them to do as educator Lauren Zucker (2016) recommends: "'Read small,' paying attention to details, noticing and tracking patterns, and making connections, so that [you] can later 'think big' about deeper meanings" (p. 92). Then I offer some of Zucker's (2016) other ideas for future reference:

- Use a squiggly underline to indicate there's something important going on, even if you're not sure what it means.
- Box new characters' names, because authors often introduce characters with revealing details.
- Instead of underlining a long section of text, use a bracket next to that section and write your thoughts beside it.
- Circle unfamiliar words as a cue to look them up and jot down definitions.
- Record questions, and use a question mark to indicate an idea is tentative (or start the idea with "maybe").
- Use punctuation marks such as asterisks and exclamation points to indicate important, surprising, or climactic moments.
- Draw small pictures (e.g., a heart or gravestone) or write a concise summary to mark major plot events. (p. 93)

Labeling Text With Sticky Notes

Another reading strategy I introduce to students early in the school year is how to use sticky notes to label a text for easy reference. Teachers and students alike have different feelings about using sticky notes for close reading, but I feel strongly that I must at least introduce this strategy so students can make an informed decision about whether it works for them. I check these sticky notes for completion, and allow for individual differences in execution. If teachers encourage students to use sticky notes with some flexibility, the strategy becomes more than a simple exercise in compliance, and becomes just one other tool in their toolbox students can use to determine if sticky notes aid in their comprehension and retention.

Offering students the opportunity to make choices about what they need as readers and learners is how "learners practice judgment, not just skill" (Wiggins, 2010). It also conveys that we accept students for who they are and support their independence and autonomy, which not only increase engagement but the likelihood of skills transfer to their lives beyond school (Ryan & Deci, 2000). We need to continually ask ourselves what skills and dispositions students still abide by when their teacher is no longer looking over their shoulder, there's no rubric, and they are not being measured and judged by a grade. The answer: it will be the skills and dispositions that work for and feel right to them.

I usually design the sticky note strategy to align with an upcoming activity or project, so students understand why teachers create this system in the first place and then ultimately students realize its efficacy. I have a simple plan for using sticky notes to satisfy the reluctant student, yet allow the more enthusiastic student room to expand. For whole-class texts, I generally ask students to place a sticky note at the beginning of each chapter with a one-sentence summary of the chapter for easy reference during book discussions and activities. Then, within the chapters, I ask students to place smaller sticky notes, depending on the area of focus. Table 4.1 lists ideas that align this philosophy across texts.

Table 4.1: Strategic Use of Sticky Notes

Focus Area	Sticky Notes in Each Chapter
Writer's style	Notice two places with an author's effective word choice, phrasing, or literary techniques, and mark each with a sticky note.
Vocabulary	When you encounter unfamiliar vocabulary words, mark at least two with sticky notes.
Character analysis	For the character you are tracking, place a sticky note when the character is present in the story or another character is talking about the character.
Themes, motifs, or symbols	Place a sticky note when you notice a recurring symbol or idea to eventually determine whether it is significant.

Analyzing Characters

One learning outcome I model with a whole-class text is the analysis of characters to deepen students' understanding of the complexities of what it means to be human. Many state standards reference this skill because it requires students to analyze characters by their words, actions, and interactions, and determine how the characters develop and affect the plot or theme. Teachers can engage students in the wonder of reading by reminding them that fiction welcomes us into people's lives and thinking in a way that isn't possible in real life. Reading fiction helps us learn lessons from a safe distance because we don't have to suffer the consequences of a character's actions or inaction. Together, we can recognize the weaknesses of the human condition, so we don't repeat the same mistakes. As novelist James Baldwin (as cited in Goodreads, n.d.c) so eloquently wrote:

> You think your pain and your heartbreak are unprecedented in the history of the world, but then you read. It was books that taught me that the things that tormented me most were the very things that connected me with all the people who were alive, who had ever been alive.

As we experience these lessons together, my students and I explore our commonalities and all the ways we are more the same than different, which further strengthens our classroom bonds. One way we analyze is through a character exploration (figure 4.2) in which each group selects a different character to track through a novel.

Directions: For this project, your group will demonstrate its understanding of a character by creating a visual representation and an in-depth analysis.

Part One: Body Map

Your group will use the planning sheet provided to create a body map of its assigned character. The body map is a visual outline of the character illustrating implicit (inferences and analysis) and explicit (quotes and textual evidence) details. Your group's choices should represent a careful analysis and a profound understanding of the character as the author develops him or her over the course of the literary work.

Planning Sheet

Character name:

Physical description: What does your character look like? In other words, what does the author explicitly state about your character's appearance?

Key quotations: Choose at least two quotations your character says that reveal his or her character.

Quote one:

Significance:

Quote two:

Significance:

Continued ▶

Figure 4.2: Character exploration template.

Key quotation spoken about your character: Choose at least one quotation that *another* character says about your character that reveals something about him or her.

Speaker:

Quote:

Significance:

Actions: What does your character do that suggests something about him or her?

Thoughts: What can you infer your character believes or thinks about?

Goals and motivations: What is the dominant, unconscious goal your character is striving for?

Principles and worst attributes (virtues and vices): What are your character's most admirable qualities? What are your character's worst qualities?

Thesis statement: Using evidence from the text, form a thesis statement or claim that explains what kind of person your character is and what motivates him or her.

Part Two: Poem

Your group will need to collaborate and write a poem to accompany its body map. Your group must write the poem in one of the following poetic types. As these poems are stylistically simplistic, your group should use vivid and complex language to express its overall meaning.

Types of Poems

Option one: Cinquain

A *cinquain* is a five-line poem that describes a person, place, or thing (ReadWriteThink, n.d.).

Line 1 has one word—a noun that tells what your poem is about.

Line 2 has two adjectives that describe what you're writing about.

Line 3 has three gerunds (-ing words) that describe what your poem is about.

Line 4 has a phrase that tells more about what you're writing about.

Line 5 has a noun—a synonym for your title that tells what your poem is about.

Option two: Haiku

"A traditional Japanese haiku is a three-line poem with seventeen syllables, written in a 5/7/5 syllable count. Often focusing on images from nature, haiku emphasizes simplicity, intensity, and directness of expression" (Poets.org, 2016).

Option three: Limerick

A limerick is a humorous rhyming poem that has five lines.

Visit **go.SolutionTree.com/literacy** for a free reproducible version of this figure.

As students are immersed in their character analyses, I get the opportunity to help them find textual evidence to support their interpretation and answer questions such as, "Why, if he loved her so much, did he repeatedly disappoint her?" and "Why did he only learn his lesson after it was too late?" I've heard them talk about their character's thoughts, feelings, and motivations and debate the character's virtues and vices. You might hear them tapping in time together to cobble together a poem, laughing and reciting to one another different witty and insightful interpretations. By design, this activity generates the kind of conversations that strengthen belonging.

Exploring Writer's Craft

Another of my students' learning outcomes is to explore and understand a writer's craft to determine how the use of language impacts readers, as well as inspires and informs our own writing. Students must identify how figurative language and connotations impact meaning and tone as well as the overall impact on the reader as referenced in many state standards.

An effective method of practicing this activity is to select a passage clearly depicting explicit craft moves that directly affect a text's overall impact. For example, a colleague inspired me to have my ninth graders annotate Juliet's soliloquy from act 4, scene 3 of *Romeo and Juliet* (Shakespeare, 1595/1997), in which she expresses her fears before drinking Friar Laurence's potion. Juliet's soliloquy is a great example because many of the words Shakespeare chooses students are familiar with, such as thrills, poison, stifled, dismal, and festering. This activity not only strengthens students' close reading skills and understanding of writer's craft, it very clearly illustrates that they have words at their disposal to make their writing even stronger simply by investing a little more time and attention.

Students use colored pencils to color code and label words with positive and negative connotations, words whose sound and rhythm contribute to meaning, and words and phrases that elicit an emotional response from them. Students also mark where they notice repetition, parallelism, imagery, and figurative language. Often, I assign particular colors to particular craft moves, so students can check their work against one another.

Students then demonstrate their understanding by selecting key words from the monologue (figure 4.3, page 84) and assembling them in a word cloud (figure 4.4, page 84) to visually depict how, even with an absence of context, the use of precise words conveys meaning. Students place these word clouds in a shared online folder and participate in a virtual gallery walk.

Directions: As you read and annotate Juliet's soliloquy in act 4, scene 3, please complete the following, including answering the questions.

- Highlight and label all examples of figurative language in the speech.
- Label words with positive or negative connotations (using a + or –).
- Label words packed with meaning (considering how they sound, the images they convey, and so on).
- What are Juliet's fears? She proposes a lot of *what if* scenarios. What kinds of things does she imagine happening?
- What is Juliet concerned about in terms of Friar Laurence and his intentions?
- What is the author's purpose in this speech, and how does he use figurative language, repetition, and word choice to establish this meaning?
- How do these word choices and imagery create a cumulative impact on the meaning and tone of Juliet's soliloquy?
- How can you use what you have learned from Shakespeare's use of language to improve your own writing?

Source: Adapted from Carolyn Hoyt, West Windsor-Plainsboro High School North.

Figure 4.3: Teaching the writer's craft.

Visit **go.SolutionTree.com/literacy** for a free reproducible version of this figure.

Source: Wordle.net, 2020.

Figure 4.4: Word cloud from Juliet's soliloquy.

Understanding Theme

I want students to understand that one of the values of reading lies in its power to teach us lessons we are often unable to readily learn in our own lives because our needs, insecurities, and vulnerabilities eclipse the truth. To illustrate this point, I share Jessamyn West's (1957) quote with students: "Fiction reveals truths that reality obscures" (p. 39).

I prompt students to analyze this quote by asking them questions such as, "How do we learn lessons through reading?" and "Why, even though these same lessons often present themselves in our real lives, are we often unable to immediately learn from them?" Students quickly begin to understand that it's easier to understand the truth and learn lessons when we have perspective and emotional distance. Teachers can apply this activity to nonfiction texts across disciplines because it asks students to recognize how central ideas form over the course of a text, which is a common state standard (figure 4.5).

Directions: Copy a quote from your book you feel reveals a universal truth. We will then randomly distribute these papers, and another student will attempt to uncover a truth your quote conveys.

Direct quotation from the text:

Truth:

Fiction examples

"Like she was trying to be pretty and popular. It was the trying part that was so disgusting." —*Eleanor & Park* (Rowell, 2013, p. 215)

Truth: It's sad how we try so hard just to be accepted.

"No one in the world ever gets what they want, and that is beautiful." —*Ready Player One* (Cline, 2011, p. 199)

Truth: If we got everything we wanted, we would have nothing to work for.

"You start believing you're poor because you're stupid and ugly. And then you start believing that you're stupid and ugly because you're Indian. . . . It's an ugly circle and there's nothing you can do about it." —*The Absolutely True Diary of a Part-Time Indian* (Alexie, 2007, p. 13)

Truth: We can be so mean to ourselves; we blame ourselves for things that are not our fault.

Continued ►

Figure 4.5: How stories reveal truth.

Nonfiction examples

"There is nothing uniquely evil in these destroyers or even in this moment. The destroyers are merely men enforcing the whims of our country, correctly interpreting its heritage and legacy." —*Between the World and Me* (Coates, 2015, p. 10)

Truth: People in power who commit unfair actions are not evil. They are following society's beliefs.

"But, on the whole, tho' I never arrived at the perfection I had been so ambitious of obtaining, but fell far short of it, yet I was, by the endeavour, a better and happier man than I otherwise should have been if I had not attempted it." —*The Autobiography of Benjamin Franklin* (Franklin, 1793/1922, p. 41)

Truth: Self-improvement is always worth attempting, even if you don't exactly reach your goal.

Visit **go.SolutionTree.com/literacy** for a free reproducible version of this figure.

Questioning

Another way my class explores the intricacies of reading is by looking at how some of the critical elements of a text work together to impact our experience as readers. This activity uses skills evident in many state standards—understand implicit and explicit meanings, analyze author's craft, and transfer the learning beyond the text. This works for fiction and nonfiction texts. My students generally do a jigsaw activity, with different groups focusing on different chapters (figure 4.6).

Directions: For each response, cite evidence from the text to support your answer.

What does the text say? In your own words, explain what the chapter is about.

How does the text work? Identify two craft moves that make the storytelling more effective. If you know what the technique is called, identify it.

Text evidence:

Literary technique:

Text evidence:

Literary technique:

What does the text mean? Choose one character or event and consider these questions: What do you think the character's words, actions, or events in this chapter might represent? What do you think these words, actions, or events are designed to teach us? Explain why you think so.

How can you relate any of the information cited from the text to your own life? Choose one character or event and consider this question: How does a character's words, actions, or events in this chapter relate to my life and my experiences?

Why does this matter? What is the purpose of analyzing a text in this way? In other words, in what ways does identifying these aspects of the text enhance your experience as a reader?

Source: Adapted from Fisher, 2016.

Figure 4.6: Comprehension-deepening template.

Visit **go.SolutionTree.com/literacy** for a free reproducible version of this figure.

One of my favorite questions to ask students about any reading is, "How are all our stories really everyone's stories?" This question makes students recognize we can all personally connect to characters across time periods, places, and cultures. This question challenges students to understand that the universality of the human experience transcends how different we may appear based on how we look, where we live, or what kind of family we have. We consistently revisit and build on this question, and then I slowly expand this idea when I ask students to consider how recognizing our common humanity relates to gratitude and personal happiness. As we see how our stories intersect, it reinforces our connectedness to one another (figure 4.7).

How are all our stories really everyone's stories? In other words, how can you relate to these characters' feelings, actions, and reactions? How does your answer show we are all more the same than different?

Answer for each character:

What part of ______________________________'s story is your story?

What part of ______________________________'s story is your story?

What part of ______________________________'s story is your story?

What part of ______________________________'s story is your story?

Continued ▶

Figure 4.7: How are all of our stories really everyone's stories?

How can trying to understand other people's perspectives enhance our understanding of ourselves and the world?

How can trying to understand other people's perspectives cause us to have more gratitude for the gifts in our own lives?

How can trying to understand other people's perspectives lead to greater personal happiness?

Visit **go.SolutionTree.com/literacy** for a free reproducible version of this figure.

Reading Independently

Although the comprehensive study of whole-class texts is essential, it is insufficient to help students develop as readers. Independent reading is crucial, and, according to Krashen (2004), "the single biggest predictor of student literacy success" (as cited in Bosworth, 2017). And yet, in "typical classrooms it is not unusual to find that kids read and write for as little as 10 percent of the day" (Allington, 2002). To motivate students to build an independent reading life, I inform my students of how essential it is for them to incorporate a regular reading routine into their lives. Students are surprised to hear reading achievement has a direct impact on students' test scores, as well as future success. As cited in a National Endowment for the Arts (2007) report, students at ages nine, thirteen, and seventeen:

> who indicated that they read for fun almost every day had higher average reading scores in 2004 than those who said that they never or hardly ever read for fun. Students at all three age levels who said that they read for fun once or twice a week had higher average scores than those who never or hardly ever read for fun. (p. 69)

Further, teenagers' independent reading is also linked to future success. A study from the University of Oxford (2011) finds, "Reading books is the only out-of-school activity for 16-year-olds that is linked to getting a managerial or professional job in later life."

My third-, fourth-, and fifth-grade teachers have all made me a better reader by just letting me read and read. —Fifth grader

To ignite students' interest in reading, teachers must include stories as varied and diverse as their students. Novelist Chimamanda Ngozi Adichie (2009) describes the importance of seeing ourselves in the stories we read in her 2009 TED Talk, "The Danger of a Single Story." Adichie (2009) says, "Because all I had read were books in which characters were foreign, I had become convinced that books by their very nature had to have foreigners in them and had to be about things with which I could not personally identify." Adichie's (2009) words remind teachers they must guide students toward books that include diverse voices, perspectives, genders, and cultures that reflect their own experiences. To foster a love of reading, students need the freedom to seek out stories that appeal to their interests, lives, and experiences. "Understanding the habits, interests, and challenges of individual readers becomes a central part of teaching. . . . We have to pull in close to our readers and listen" (Kittle, 2013, p. xv).

Author Walter Dean Myers (2014) writes about inner-city youth and people of color who are underrepresented in literature; he believes readers who love his books:

> have been struck by the recognition of themselves in the story, a validation of their existence as human beings, an acknowledgment of their value by someone who understands who they are. It is the shock of recognition at its highest level.

Teachers must acquaint students with books in which they can see their reflection, so they can have the affirmation there are other people in the world who have lived and are living lives that look and feel like their lives. Remember Brown's (2012) words: "Our sense of belonging can never be greater than our level of self-acceptance" (p. 32). The right book in the hands of the right child can build this self-acceptance.

Take your class to the school library early in the year. The librarian can pull high-interest books for students to browse through, or they can check the shelves for some of their favorite authors. Students can work in pairs to review books, and then leave the library with a completed reading list (figure 4.8, page 90) and at least one checked-out book each.

I further support independent reading in my class by devoting twenty minutes once a week to choice reading. It may not seem like much, but it conveys to students that reading books of their choice matters enough for me to carve out time for them to do it during class time. I generally insist students read analog books or e-readers to avoid the distraction of phones or laptops, but I make an exception for the few students who are passionate about reading fanfiction or who are engrossed in a particular webtoon (digital comic). I want to support them as readers, and I want them to enjoy this time!

Of course, in a classroom where students may be reading different books, assessment questions arise. Choice reading is critical to developing readers, but it is messy, and the assessment must be as expansive and imperfect as the business of books themselves. When it comes to assessing choice reading, I check journal entries, conference with students, and assign activities students can use across texts for book clubs and independent reading, or I assign a written reflection as a culminating assignment (figure 4.9, pages 91–92). I also think sometimes teachers just need to reconcile the fact that they don't need to assess everything students do. How about just reading for the sake of reading?

The way we can nurture ourselves as readers is to have a ready reserve of books we are interested in reading. The librarian has selected a variety of books ranging from fiction to nonfiction and graphic novel to literary classic.

Step one: You and your partner will *each* select a book to preview. During your preview, you will do the following.

- Look at the front cover.
- Read the back of the book.
- Flip through the book to notice the font size, chapter length, and any other interesting features.
- Read the first paragraph or two.

Step two: *Without discussing the books*, quietly switch books and repeat step one with your partner's book.

Step three: Do the following.

- Talk about the books one at a time. You might want to flip through the pages to discuss the features you noticed.
- If you're interested in one or both books, add the titles and details to your reading library by filling in the form provided.
- Return to step one and repeat the process!

Your goal is to preview between twelve and fifteen books and add at least eight books to your reading library.

My Reading Library		
Title	**Author**	**Reasons I Want to Read It** Summarize what the book is about and name one other detail that explains why the book appeals to you.

Figure 4.8: Developing a reading list.

Visit **go.SolutionTree.com/literacy** for a free reproducible version of this figure.

Directions: You will write a one or two-page formal reflection about how the book you selected affected you. *You must respond to the prompts*, but you can expand your focus by responding to one or more of the following guiding questions.

How did your book change your view of yourself or the world?

Writer's purpose:

Writer's role:

Audience:

Genre (novel, graphic novel, or the like):

Form (hard copy, e-reader, audiobook):

Consider these questions as you write your reflection.

- Did you identify with one of the characters in the novel? If so, how and why?
- Did the book reveal a universal truth you made a personal connection to or help deepen your understanding about life?
- Can the book be viewed in a larger context as a social criticism?
- Did this experience of selecting a book and reading independently change your view of yourself as a reader?
- How did your experience as a participant in your book discussions deepen your understanding of your book or how books can enhance conversations and connections between people?
- As a reader and a student, do you prefer independent reading or whole-class reading of novels or plays? Explain the benefits and drawbacks of each.

You should cite *textual evidence* from the book as well as from your discussions and your own life. The more details and examples you provide, the more effective your reflection will be. Your closing remarks should convey to your reader the broader significance of what you learned from your book as well as your book discussions, and express to the reader why it matters. You should provide context about your book, but avoid summarizing it.

Assessment: I will grade your paper on the following for a total of 30 points.

Format and content: ____/20

- Interesting, insightful response to the prompt using specific examples from discussions or the text: ____/10
- At least two well-chosen quotations from the novel seamlessly integrated into the reflection to make a direct, meaningful connection: ____/4
- Creative, interesting title: ____/1
- Clear topic sentence and closing sentences: ____/3
- Properly formatted heading, font, and type size: ____/1

Continued ▶

Figure 4.9: Reading reflection.

- Two or three pages: ____/1

Writing style: ____/10

- Clarity, precision: ____/4
- Organization, progression of ideas: ____/2
- Style, descriptiveness, word choice: ____/2
- Knowledge of language and conventions: ____/2

Source: Adapted from Collins, 2007.

Visit **go.SolutionTree.com/literacy** for a free reproducible version of this figure.

Even when I don't formally grade, I incorporate reflection throughout our experiences as readers so students can consolidate and make sense of what they learn. Sometimes students process what they learn through paired and small-group discussions, short stop-and-jots, or longer entries. Through written reflection, students more deeply consider character, theme, and conflict, as well as controversial issues helping them solidify what they've learned, and it drives further conversation (figure 4.10).

Directions: Answer the following questions.

- So what?
- Who cares?
- Why is this issue significant or worth considering?
- What other questions do I have?

Figure 4.10: Questions for reflection and further conversation.

Visit **go.SolutionTree.com/literacy** for a free reproducible version of this figure.

Reading Like a Historian

In the history department at West Windsor-Plainsboro Regional School District, supervisor Carl Cooper advocates using and adapting lessons, reading protocols, and rubrics from the Stanford History Education Group (SHEG; https://sheg.stanford.edu), which are available to download for free.

Among other varied resources, SHEG offers rubrics designed to teach students how to critically read nonfiction texts and primary source documents. The rubric begins with source questions such as, "Who wrote this, when, and why?" Other questions cue students to identify historical context, as well as related texts or documents that existed at the time. It also includes close reading strategies designed to help students identify the author's claim, analyze writing style, and ultimately draw a conclusion about the author's perspective.

The ability to understand the explicit and implicit meaning of nonfiction texts is a common state standard, and students can apply these close reading techniques to nonfiction texts across disciplines to foster critical skills. SHEG's strategies and lessons teach students not only reading strategies, but also the kinds of questions to ask as critical thinkers, which will improve their overall literacy skills and help them become thoughtful citizens (C. Cooper, personal communication, November 14, 2019).

While Students Are Working

While students are working, it is helpful for the teacher to offer them as much feedback as possible. Wiggins (2012) reminds teachers:

> Although the universal teacher lament that there's no time for such feedback is understandable, remember that "no time to give and use feedback" actually means "no time to cause learning." As we have seen, research shows that *less* teaching plus *more* feedback is the key to achieving greater learning.

What does feedback look like when the goal is to help students grow as readers?

If teachers model reading instruction according to what reading looks like in real life, they should have many conversations with students about the books they are reading. Since throughout the year, students will read different books, individual conferences can serve as a powerful formative assessment tool. During these conferences, teachers can offer feedback and help students set further reading goals and, through informal conversations, teachers can strengthen personal relationships with students.

Feedback offered to nurture students as readers must be freed from the constraints of formal assessment. Conversations with students about books should center on mutually sharing significant passages and relating the text to one's own life, other disciplines, and real-world issues. We should discuss characters, question the author's motivation for stylistic choices, and wonder why a segment ended the way it did. If during guided instruction you model what conversations about reading sound like, individual conferences present the opportunity for students to take the lead using scaffolding you provide. All conferences have a successful outcome because students arrive prepared to have a meaningful one-to-one conversation with their teacher of their own design.

Choosing books for book clubs taught me to love reading. It is always interesting to pick the books that appeal to you and to see who else shares your interests. The ability to read books that I like showed me how much books can mean and how much I can learn. —Seventh grader

I generally ask students to arrive to our conferences prepared with what they'd like to talk about (figure 4.11).

Mark a passage in your book to share, and be prepared to explain why you like it, what it reveals, and how it connects to the text as a whole. Here are some to choose from; they'll guide our conversation.

- Discuss a character you find intriguing. Piece together textual evidence of what the character says and does, and what other characters say about him or her.
- Share a quote from the text you think reveals a truth about life, and explain your understanding and how it relates to your life.
- Share a unique feature about the book and explain how you feel it's effective or ineffective. Is it the narrator or narrators of the book? The chapter organization or length? A particular description of a scene or character?
- What is your most favorite or least favorite part of the book? Can you share a section and explain why you think so?
- Is there a part of the book you find confusing? Can you share part of that section and explain what in particular about it is confusing?

Figure 4.11: Student conference-preparation ideas.

Visit **go.SolutionTree.com/literacy** for a free reproducible version of this figure.

Whether students are reading choice books or whole-class texts, during small-group book discussions, teachers can monitor students' understanding by carefully listening to their thoughts and insights and joining conversations to probe their thinking and deepen the discussion. When students are working on completing a handout, it can be helpful to designate a particular space or box for them to record a pivotal response or a conclusion so when circulating, you can quickly assess for understanding. If you notice a pattern of incorrect or surface responses, you can call them to the class's attention, offer feedback, and provide questions to guide students to think more deeply and correct any misconceptions before students move further.

Teachers can also assess individual understanding midpoint through a lesson to quickly determine if they need to reteach certain concepts. For example, if your primary learning outcome is for students to understand the literal meaning of a challenging primary source document or Shakespearean text, you might conduct one quick digital survey (such as Kahoot! or a Google Form) that has only one correct answer. Those real-time data let you know if the class is ready to move on to deeper analysis or if the whole class or some students still need more guided instruction on basic comprehension. As often as possible, teachers should assess students' progress in real time, so students receive timely, meaningful feedback and teachers can adjust instruction accordingly.

Second Chances and Do-Overs

A failed reading quiz, an off-base summary, or an unsupported literary analysis are so much more than the resulting grade—they provide valuable information. Teachers need to ask students questions like: "What happened? How do you think you can do better?" along with the follow-up statement, "Let's figure it out together." A failed reading quiz likely means the student just didn't read. If that's the case, I assure them it's OK and that not reading doesn't make them bad people nor does it make me like them any less. But then I do ask, "What will you do differently next time?" When students insist they are reading but are still performing unsuccessfully, we need to intervene individually by reviewing the assessment with the student and finding the issue. One method is by asking the student to read a passage with questions to identify if there is an underlying comprehension issue. It is not uncommon for students to arrive in the secondary grades with undiagnosed learning differences. There is always time for an intervention and a second chance.

If a student honestly misinterprets a text, the teacher's role becomes to determine what happened during the construction of the summary or analysis. It is only then the teacher can advise the student to select the proper tool or strategy to improve his or her performance on the next task. When it comes to offering second chances in reading, I make a case-by-case determination on what exactly needs to be redone, and how I will re-evaluate the student. I determine the following.

- What does the student most need to learn?
- What part of the task will cause learning?
- What will motivate the student to fully engage?

It is cumbersome to have students resubmit old assignments. However, teachers cannot overlook misinterpretations of texts or allow students to move forward using the same faulty tools or incorrect reasoning. Students' proficiency and continued growth as readers are far too consequential:

> Although we can't do it 100 percent of the time, allowing students to redo both assignments and assessments for particularly important standards and outcomes *most* of the time

> is highly effective. This approach reflects what we know about successful learning, and it better prepares students for the world beyond school. (Wormeli, 2011)

I once had a student who, on a reading assessment, misunderstood the character's intentions from the very beginning, and then interpreted and analyzed the remainder of the text based on the initial misconception. Fortunately, teachers can create opportunities for second chances. These do-overs not only show compassion to students, build trust, and strengthen relationships, but these second chances are how we learn.

My design technology teacher in my senior year has given me a lot of help figuring out whether I want to go to college or not, and why I should go. This made a big difference in my life because he has convinced me that college is worth the time. —Twelfth grader

---

According to the National Commission on Writing in America's Schools and Colleges (2003):

> If students are to make knowledge their own, they must struggle with the details, wrestle with the facts, and rework raw information and dimly understood concepts into language they can communicate to someone else. In short, if our student readers are to learn, they must also write. (p. 9)

In the next chapter, we'll explore how a dynamic and thriving reading life can support students' journeys as writers.

Questions for Reflection

Consider these questions after reading the chapter.

Do I balance whole-class texts and independent choice reading? If not, how can I improve the balance?

____

____

In what ways am I satisfied with my current reading instruction, and in what ways can I improve?

____

____

How can I implement ideas from this chapter to more effectively develop students as readers?

____

____

How can I incorporate more student choice in my classroom to help students develop into lifelong readers?

____

____

That you are here—that life exists and identity,/ That the powerful play goes on, and you may contribute a verse.

—Walt Whitman

Developing Writers

Students need time to write so they can figure out difficult concepts, clarify their thoughts, synthesize multiple theories or ideas, and reflect on their own learning. Schmoker (2006) writes, "With reading as its raw material, writing exercises the intellect as it moves from amorphous understanding toward precision and practical application" (p. 64). However, many of my students don't value writing nearly as much as they do some of their other subjects. They seem to think that problem solving and experimentation are what real learning looks like, while writing is somehow less important. In *Results Now*, a critique of literacy education in the United States, Schmoker (2006) contends that a "deeper look at writing reveals its impact on our ability to learn and think at the highest levels, across the disciplines. Writing literally makes students smarter" (p. 62). According to the National Commission on Writing in America's Schools and Colleges (2003), "If students are to learn, they must write" (p. 9).

To me, it's even more than that. When students write, even if they don't reach a correct response or a satisfying conclusion, they acknowledge their thoughts and give them life. Nye (as cited in Tippett, 2018d) expresses, "Very rarely do you hear people say that they write things down and feel worse. . . . It is an act that helps you, preserves you, energizes you in the very doing of it." Writer Joan Didion (1976) says, "I write entirely to find out what I'm thinking."

The problem is, writing well does not come naturally for everyone, and as our own worst critics, we are reluctant to perform tasks that we don't do well. Yet, to think through writing, to write as an emotional release, and to write as a transformative act do not require that we are a master at our craft. The benefits we gain from writing are equally available to all of us. For some of my students, the ink from their pens flows with ease to fill up a page in ten minutes, while other students sit staring at a mostly blank page as they agonize to transform their thoughts into words. I remind them this is OK; it is not a race. I assure them that over time, with repeated practice, their stamina will increase and the words will come. I tell everyone to write how you talk, and your thoughts will appear on the page.

Stanford University Professor David Labaree (2018) says, "Learning to write is extraordinarily difficult, and teaching people how to write is just as hard." It stands to reason that my student readers are my strongest writers. These students' minds are swirling with metaphors, colors, and inspiration. Weaker writers not only lack the richness in language, but also they just don't engage in the repeated practice required to improve their writing. The frustrating reality about writing instruction is if students somehow are not improving, there is a very strong possibility teachers have no idea why.

Yet, I firmly believe students can grow into better writers. Even in an average paper, there is at least one clever phrase, thought-provoking observation, and maybe even a perspective I hadn't considered. These observations give me hope, and I think my consistent assurance helps my students remain hopeful as well. Fortunately, our classroom culture mitigates some of their angst, as there is no dress code for this "come-as-you-are party" (Lamott, 2018a, p. 180).

In this chapter, we will look at how teachers can plan backward as they seek to answer the question, Who do we want our students to be as writers? I also offer ideas and strategies for immediate use with the potential to help students become better writers as the writing process strengthens relationships and solidifies students' sense of belonging.

Writing in a Learner-Centered Classroom

As teachers, we should offer students choices about what they write, so they can invest in the process. In a learner-centered classroom, students must be responsible for their own learning, and the teacher's role is to create the conditions for them to thrive. After all, "You only really learn when you are excited or interested" (Stanford Graduate School of Education, 2018). Students buy in, and engagement is especially important in writing instruction. That is true because, unlike many other subjects, writing offers no worksheet, lab report, or equation to solve. We are quite literally offering students a blank page with the expectation that they have the capacity to create something others can read. Well-established teacher-student relationships and a sense of belonging support and guide students on the path to become better writers.

My digital production and audio engineering teacher taught me that writing music comes from your emotions and your imagination. He taught me that you need to feel the music, not just hear it. You need to listen with your body, not just your ears, and you need to write it carefully as if it were poetry, not just scribble things onto a piece of paper.
—Twelfth grader

Once students embark on this writing journey, the steps they take and the directions they turn will vary, but they can all use the provided tools, resources, guidance, and support as they carve their own path. If students know the teacher values them, only has their best interests in mind, and will support them when they struggle, students will follow the teacher's lead even when the road becomes difficult. Educator and author Scott Korb (2018) writes in "The Soul-Crushing Student Essay":

> First, we need to value more the complete and complex lives of young people. . . . They have already lived lives worthy of our attention and appreciation. Second, we need to encourage young people to take seriously those lives they've lived . . . . Through this, we can help them learn to expect more of themselves, too.

There is no cookie-cutter format or one-size-fits-all model to develop student writers. Teachers should embolden students to draw on the complexities, richness, and diversity of their lives' experiences to flourish as writers. Students, in turn, must know we are interested in what they have to say and that we are here, eager to read their words. They need to know that we are listening.

To Begin

I want students to write in different forms and styles for a variety of purposes and audiences; to know the value of risk-taking, multiple drafts, and feedback; and to understand writing gets better with repeated practice (similar to mastering any other skill). Teachers want students to understand the value of writing as a means to clarify thinking, reflect on experiences, and convey thoughts clearly through attentiveness to words and language (State of New Jersey Department of Education, n.d.).

My third-grade teacher had one-on-one conferences every couple of days to help us become better writers. She gave me constructive criticism while, at the same time, recognized the parts of my writing that she believed were my strengths. She would make sure to point out how much my writing had improved since the last time I saw her. It excited me to know that my hard work was making a difference. —Ninth grader

Writing is a beautiful entanglement of skill, craft, thought, and emotion driven by motivation and inspiration. I've curated a list of ten writing tips, culled from "13 Writing Tips, From Beloved Teacher Anne Lamott," and generally ask students to quietly read them with a highlighter in hand:

> There's no shame in hitting the "delete" button.
>
> Your first draft will stink—and that's OK.
>
> Find a couple of critics you love.
>
> Imagine the book you dream of finding, and then bring it to life.
>
> You'll get so much more out of writing than just a manuscript.
>
> It will probably take some trial and error before you find your voice as a writer.
>
> Don't wait to be "in the mood" to write—unless you want to wait forever.
>
> Waste more time *and* more paper.
>
> Try to be your own coach.
>
> Think of your writing as a gift to the world. (Lamott, 2017a)

The students' goal is to look for one or two tips that connect to their experiences as writers, discuss the resonating ideas with other group members, and explain how the tips relate to their personal writing experiences. Sometimes, I ask students to share a few of their reflections with the whole class so other students can hear what their peers are thinking. Sometimes I ask students to write the tips that speak to them either in the front inside of their writer's notebook or in a Google Doc they use for Quotes of the Week (Do Now activity, page 66). I remind students all of us can use daily inspirational reminders.

Teachers can't stress to students enough that if they don't allow themselves to write badly, they will never write anything at all. Since we approach writing as a process, students write more than they need to and "press the delete button" shamelessly and often. In class, we often use the phrase *writing opportunity* rather than *writing assignment*, and *last draft* instead of *final draft*. Some students tease me because these names don't change anything, but words matter. These delineations serve as reminders to students that their writing is never really finished, and help them forgive themselves for the imperfections in their last drafts, paving the way for feedback.

Lamott (1994) talks extensively throughout her books about writing and being a writer, and I share with my students her philosophy from *Bird by Bird: Some Instructions on Writing and Life* about terrible first drafts. In Lamott's (1994) beloved story about her father's advice to her ten-year-old brother, who was overwhelmed at the prospect of writing his report on birds, she writes:

> He was at the kitchen table, close to tears, surrounded by binder paper and pencils and unopened books on birds, immobilized by the hugeness of the task ahead. Then my father sat down beside him, put his arm around my brother's shoulder, and said, "Bird by bird, buddy. Just take it bird by bird." (p. 19)

Students need to take ownership of their journey to improve as writers, and when students write about what matters to them, their writing suddenly has meaning to them. Teachers can shift the responsibility of learning to the student by following the gradual release of responsibility model (Fisher & Frey, 2014). Following this model, I explain and model what I'd like students to do (*I do*), offer an opportunity for us to practice together (*we do*), shift the responsibility of the task to them (*you do it together*), and when they appear to be ready, they can begin working independently (*you do it*; Fisher & Frey, 2014).

I generally use this model to begin writing opportunities as well as each time I introduce a new concept or skill. For example, when we begin writing first-person monologues from a character's perspective to think about a character's motivation, I introduce the idea that every person—even these characters—has a voice inside his or her own head that tells us things about ourselves that may or may not be true. I have offered that my internal voice constantly reminds me that I'm not very coordinated and so it inhibits me, if I allow it, to stay off the dance floor, refrain from faculty volleyball games, and stay in the back of exercise class. Then, I ask students to share in their groups what the voices inside their heads tell them and how this affects their behavior.

During this *we do* (Fisher & Frey, 2014), I listen in on group conversations and sometimes interject if students are off track. Then, I call for a whole-class pause and shift the groups' conversations to consider the thoughts of one of the characters we are familiar with. I listen in again, and once students clearly understand what I mean about investigating a character's interior life, they are ready to begin their independent work. During this last stage, I offer questions and prompts to guide their thinking further, and I assist students who need additional support. It "is through this process of gradually assuming more and more responsibility for their learning that students become competent, independent learners" (Graves & Fitzgerald, 2003, p. 98).

Finally, students are forever wondering: "Why are we learning this?" and "When are we ever going to use this?" I explain how all their required writing skills apply far beyond English class. For example, students may have to explain their rationale in a chemistry lab or explain their work on a mathematics problem. They may need to write a persuasive email or a compelling paragraph on a college essay or job application—or may need to in the future. It will always be to their benefit in life to try to understand other people's thoughts and perspectives. And they may just realize the act of reflective writing can be cathartic.

Writing Activities

When contemplating student-writing lessons in a learner-centered classroom, teachers should consider how to provide complex tasks that demand practicing a myriad of skills. These tasks should incorporate choice, be relevant to students' lives and, wherever possible, be for an authentic audience beyond the classroom. Although some of these tasks might be too difficult for students, Harvard University professor Jal Mehta (2018) advances the notion that teachers don't have to teach the basics before students can engage in deeper learning. This is similar to how children play sports like Little League (Perkins, 2009), which "engenders motivation, which is what provides the fuel to practice the parts." The idea is that within these interesting and complex tasks, students will be more motivated to engage more deeply in the research to make sure their claims are accurate and well founded, to tinker with their word choices, and commit to writing more convincingly so their voices will be heard. Students who are invested in their final product will ask thoughtful questions and accept critical feedback because they care about their final product well beyond a grade. Consider the following writing activities.

Reflective Writing

The early and last stages of writing often take place in students' writer's notebooks. In my classes, we begin brainstorming ideas with bulleted lists and responding to thought-provoking prompts, and end with reflections about the process and product, along with ideas about how to proceed. With some exceptions (like for students who have a physical need to type instead of write with a pen), my classes use composition notebooks for prewriting and reflective writing. Writing by hand forces students to slow down, and quiet contemplation in the absence of keyboard clicks creates the space and the mindset for student reflection. A study by psychologists Pam A. Mueller and Daniel M. Oppenheimer (as cited in May, 2014) indicates that "if we want students to synthesize material, draw inferences, see new connections, evaluate evidence, and apply concepts in novel situations, we need to encourage the deep, effortful cognitive processes that underlie these abilities." It is through writing and stillness that we can drown out the noise of others, and begin to understand ourselves.

In September, students write with a marker on the inside cover of their composition notebooks: "I have the right to write badly in this notebook" (Spandel, as cited in Collins, 2007, p. 2). When teachers give students time to write, students can nod and think, "Yes, that makes sense now" or realize, "Oh, that happened." And even though students may not fully understand, they've recognized their thoughts and given them shape. Reflective writing strengthens students' connection to themselves, which better helps them forge relationships with others.

In addition, although the writer's notebooks encourage informal and imperfect writing, it still meets a common state standard requiring students to regularly write for different purposes, tasks, and audiences.

My third-grade teacher helped me academically. She helped me with writing because she always let me write about sports because she knew that I liked sports. That helped me a lot because I actually enjoyed doing that. —Fifth grader

---

Each marking period, I keep a running record of all writer's notebook entries in a Google Classroom (https://classroom.google.com) document, providing a quick reference for students who are absent or for those who need to finish their entries beyond the allotted class time (figure 5.1, pages 106–107). Having a dedicated space for reflection and multiple (but organized) avenues for responses provides just enough structure and flexibility to achieve our objectives while honoring and respecting each student's voice and thoughts.

Because their entries remain private, students feel less inhibited as they explore their ideas, clarify their thinking, or reflect on their progress or performance. If I, as their teacher, ever intend to ask students to share from their journals, I inform them before they begin writing and give them time to select the sentence or two they would like to share. It can be worthwhile for students to read aloud what they've managed to figure out, and for my more reticent students, it encourages participation and increases their confidence as they read aloud the thoughts they've clarified and rehearsed. The act of journal writing supports students to be brave enough to practice vulnerability and explore their own inner lives as it helps them grow into more proficient readers, writers, and thinkers.

Directions: Use your writer's notebook this year to capture your ideas on paper. Each entry should have a specific focus and fulfill the length requirement. Questions, guesses, lists, and random ideas are permissible. The goal is to create a wealth of ideas you can use for future discussions, projects, writing assignments, and overall academic growth.

I will grade your writer's notebook for completion once during a marking period. A current list of entries is available in Google Classroom.

Marking Period One Entries			
#	**Date**	**Title and Prompt**	**Requirements**
1		**Letters About Literature: Prewriting** **Title:** **Author:** Why did I choose this work? How did it change my view of myself or the world? What can I say right now that is true for me? Why am I writing this letter? What is my *central purpose*? What is the one thing I truly want to convey? Why do I want to write a letter to this author? What do I most want the author to know? How do I want the author to think or feel after reading my letter?	One full page
2		**The Enduring Value of Reading** Write down each quote in your notebook and demonstrate your understanding of each quote by explaining its meaning. Then, choose one of the following statements from "Don't Turn Away From the Art of Life" by Brown University professor Arnold Weinstein (2016) and explain how you realized this truth through a specific experience you've had as a reader.	Copy each quotation. Between five and seven sentences

		Quotes: *"'How much do you know about Shakespeare?' I once asked a friend who has committed much of her life to studying the Bard. She replied, 'Not as much as he knows about me.' Remember this the next time someone tells you literature is useless."* *"We enter the bookstore, see the many volumes arrayed there, and think: so much to read, so little time. But books do not take time; they give time, they expand our resources of both heart and mind. It may sound paradoxical, but they are, in the last analysis, scientific, for they trace the far-flung route by which we come to understand our world and ourselves."*	
3		**Final Book Club: How Stories Reveal Truth in ____________** *(Title of Your Book)* Respond to one or more of the following prompts or quotes until you reach a full page of writing. **Prompts:** How is this story in another place and time somehow about me? How do effective writers hook and hold their readers, and what does this have to do with stories revealing truth? How do books that reveal universal truths have the power to change us? What specifically about your novel felt real to you and revealed a universal truth? **Quotes:** *"You should live several lives while reading." —William Styron (as cited in BrainyQuote, n.d.)* *"Books are the quietest and most constant of friends; they are the most accessible and wisest of counselors, and the most patient of teachers." —Charles W. Eliot (as cited in Goodreads, n.d.a)* *"Books are my friends, my companions. They make me laugh and cry and find meaning in life." —Christopher Paolini (as cited in Goodreads, n.d.b)* *"There is no intellectual equivalent to allowing oneself the time and space to get lost in another person's mind, because in so doing we find ourselves." —Charles M. Blow, 2014*	One full page

Figure 5.1: Sample writer's notebook entries.

Visit **go.SolutionTree.com/literacy** for a free reproducible version of this figure.

I've struggled with how to grade these notebooks. Ideally, I'd like to not grade them at all. But it is school, and students not only expect grades but are also motivated by grades. At this point, I have decided to trust my instinct—my students' writing is valuable whether or not I read it. As Schmoker's (2006, p. 62) assertion, "Writing literally makes students smarter" reminds me, I don't need to feel guilty for not reading students' journals. I also share this idea with students: "Do you know that the act of writing literally makes you smarter?" Sometimes when they begin writing and the room becomes quiet, I'll say, "Look! You're getting smarter right now!"

I've settled on grading these notebooks for completion using the basic grading sheet in figure 5.2; the points add up to one hundred, but in my class it is a twelve-point assignment. Each marking period, I conference with each student, and flip through the pages just slowly enough to check them for completion. Together, we check the boxes on the grading sheet, and this process is sufficient to hold students accountable.

Category	Description	Not at all (0) 0%	Not really (2.25) 75%	Yes (3) 100%
Completion	All of the required entries for the marking period are complete.			
Length	Each entry meets the guidelines and length requirements.			
Organization	Each entry is clearly labelled with the appropriate title. Entries are written in a bound composition notebook (or something comparable).			
Effort	Organization, time spent, and thoughtful entries show care is evident.			

Figure 5.2: Writer's notebook assessment form.

Visit **go.SolutionTree.com/literacy** for a free reproducible version of this figure.

Generally, almost all students earn full credit on their journals. Those who do not earn full credit accept their grade with grace because the conference with me makes them fully aware of where they fell short and why. Of course, without actually reading each entry, it is impossible to ascertain each entry's level of effort or thoughtfulness. However, after we've reviewed the criteria together, the effort grade becomes clear to both the student and me. Journals that meet the first three criteria clearly show effort, and it declines from there. The form does not account for handwriting, because artful handwriting is not a prerequisite for thinking.

Perhaps most important, the individual conferences give me the opportunity to engage in conversation with each student. I generally project a few conversation starters on the overhead of what we might discuss, so students can think about these options in advance. (Refer back to figure 4.11, page 94, for general teacher-student conference prompts.) This advanced planning makes our time together more productive, plus the conferences go more swiftly.

I flip through the notebook during these conferences as the student initiates the conversation. If the notebook somehow falls short of the requirements, we discuss it together, settle on a grade, and promptly continue our conversation. My students generate the discussion based on their needs and concerns, and I listen and respond. These one-on-one interactions with students are the single most effective way to continually strengthen relationships.

Another worthwhile opportunity for reflective writing is to create the space for students to reflect deeply about children's books, young adult books, spoken word poetry, and class texts that have changed them; it opens the door to meaningful conversations between students. The Library of Congress used to hold a Letters About Literature writing contest for students in grades 4–12, which opened this door for students. Although the contest is no longer held, the work as a purposeful writing activity remains intact. Students choose a book, poem, or speech and write to the author (living or dead) about how his or her work changed the student's view of him- or herself or the world. Often, a favorite book isn't one that changed our view of ourselves or the world, so choosing an author can be difficult.

As students share books and reading passages, memories surface about special classes, favorite teachers, grandparents, well-loved toys, and times long forgotten. Books that resonate with one student often have meaning for others, albeit it in a different way; the conversations burst with life, and ideas lead to more ideas. These conversations foster our sense of belonging to ourselves as well as our connections to each other. Sometimes it is easy to pick a favorite literary work, but more difficult to choose a writer or a speaker to whom you have something to say.

Then, I remembered when I was a new teacher, more seasoned teachers would tell me to walk the walk if I was going to talk the talk. This advice might seem mundane or unnecessary, but as a new teacher, it helped me remember how closely my students follow my lead. In keeping with this advice, it seemed perfectly clear that the best way to help students choose an author and a literary work was for me to do the same. After careful thought, I realized that with all the books I had read, the author I wanted to write to was a teacher who had given a TED Talk that changed me.

I began modeling the process by inviting students into my thinking with a think-aloud. I asked what they remembered about teachers they liked as I wrote on the whiteboard: "I liked this teacher because . . ." These responses primed students to understand why I chose to write my letter to someone who inspired me. I offered students some questions to ask themselves so they can write not just to an author whose book they loved but also to someone whom they really had something to say.

- "What do I have to say to this author?"
- "How did his or her work change my view of myself or the world?"
- "What is my central purpose in writing this letter?"
- "What is the one thing that I truly want to convey?"
- "What do I want the author to do, think, or feel as a result of my writing?"
- "How could a reader connect to my experience? In other words, how does the lesson I learned have a universal quality that others can relate to?"

I offer model responses to these questions and then share Pierson's (2013) TED Talk and my sample letter, along with specific focus questions for students to use to critique my letter.

- Do you think I accurately conveyed my feelings to the author?
- Does my letter sound honest and heartfelt?
- Why do you think I felt so strongly about writing to this person?
- Did I select worthwhile quotations from the text to include in the letter?
- Which stylistic choices in my letter were effective?
- What parts of the letter need to be revised or edited? Do you have any specific suggestions?
- In what ways did I share universal feelings and ideas a reader who doesn't share my unique experience could connect to?

I assure students that my letter is a draft, and all my self-esteem doesn't rest on this single letter. I want them to feel emboldened to offer comments and criticism using questions like the following as a guide. Visit **go.SolutionTree.com/literacy** for a free reproducible version of my letter and a peer editing form.

After students share their feedback, in keeping with the gradual release of responsibility model (Fisher & Frey, 2014), I further shift the responsibility of the learning to students. Students select and analyze former winning student letters from the Library of Congress Letters About Literature archives (www.read.gov/letters) and answer many of the same questions they use to analyze my letter. Students note where the letters are effective and where they fall short as they gather ideas for their own letters (figure 5.3).

Directions: Print, highlight, and annotate the letter you selected. As you read, note in the margins the rhetorical techniques and other details you feel add to the letter's effectiveness. Then, complete the following information and staple the annotated letter to the back of this sheet.

Letter writer's name and location:

Prize and year:

Title and author of literary work:

Some techniques to look for:

- Allusions
- Pathos
- Repetition
- Personal connections
- Parallelism
- Direct quotations from the book
- Imagery

Analysis and Reflection

How does the letter writer share universal feelings and ideas a reader who doesn't share the letter writer's unique experience could connect to?

Choose three specific details from the letter and copy them here. Then, explain why you think each of these details is effective.

Figure 5.3: Letters About Literature student analysis sheet template.

Visit **go.SolutionTree.com/literacy** for a free reproducible version of this figure.

Students share excerpts from these letters by typing selected phrases into an editable Google Doc I project on a SMART Board. For each example, students note why the excerpt is effective and how it speaks to an audience beyond the book author. I strive to help students understand that if they can find the essence of why someone else's work changed them, their letter will resonate with an even larger audience, which is what we hope to do with all of our writing. Once students select a book for themselves, I meet with each individually to discuss what he or she chose and how he or she plans to answer the question, How did this author's work change your view of yourself or the world?

When students are more invested in the outcome, they ask better questions, scrutinize words and sentences, solicit more feedback, and continually self-assess. The level of contemplation required to perform this task well and the conversations that emerge as a result help us get to know one another on a deeper level. Since these letters often comprise some of the best student writing of the school year, I've had students share favorite excerpts through different media. We've completed tables in a shared Google document, a slide in a shared Google presentation, and put markers to poster paper. I've even encouraged some students who wrote exceptional letters to send their letter to the authors. Some authors respond. This writing opportunity meets many state standards because it requires students to identify a central idea from a text and write for a particular task, purpose, and audience.

Writing Contests

All writing assignments in my class offer some element of student choice and, whenever possible, students write for authentic audiences beyond our classroom. Writing contests generally fulfill many of the requirements for complex writing tasks and are relevant to students' lives. These contests motivate my students to put more time and effort into their writing because they know their voices will be heard by the world beyond our classroom. These assignments model the power of writing in a way that cannot be replicated.

When students write for an authentic audience about an issue that matters to them, by extension they suddenly care about sophisticated rhetorical moves, carefully selecting their words and crafting strong rebuttals. When they really want to effect change, they willingly read articles on the topic, watch TED Talks, and contemplate the other side of the issue with curiosity and incredulity.

I feel my teacher in sixth grade helped me a lot to break out of my shell and experiment. She helped me become a better writer because I could freely write about things that meant something to me. —Ninth grader

---

The New York Times' Learning Network (www.nytimes.com/section/learning) offers teenagers various contests (from editorial writing to photojournalism) throughout the year, and the Scholastic Art & Writing Awards (www.artandwriting.org) provide multigenre writing opportunities for students in grades 7–12. A quick online search leads to a myriad of authentic writing opportunities for student writers.

Many writing contest opportunities come with clear guidelines, instructional strategies, student exemplars, and rubrics. *The New York Times'* Learning Network Editorial Contest is an authentic opportunity to learn about argumentative writing. The contest provides students 401 prompts for argumentative writing, and a webinar helps teachers guide their students through the process. In addition, teachers who implement the contest in their classroom submit lesson plans and ideas to the Learning Network for other teachers to use.

I use these resources to help students get started in their writer's notebooks, asking them to jot down between eight and ten ideas that resonate with them after reading the prompts adapted from Kabby Hong (2017). Then they respond to at least three of the following questions, focus on one of the issues they've identified, and write down two ways they could possibly change another person's thinking.

- What issues are you struggling with?
- What are you passionate about? What are the issues in your passion?
- When you look at our society today, what makes you worried or mad?
- When you look at your generation, what makes you worried or mad?
- What do you get that other people just don't seem to get?

Author, consultant, and coach John J. Collins (2007) offers an adaptable writing assignment. Teachers can guide students to identify the assignment and its rationale; students' role, purpose, and audience; and the format in which they will be writing. I assess students on what Collins (2007) calls the focus correction areas, along with the procedure I have asked them to follow. Collins's (2007) templates are comprehensive, consistent, and user friendly, and with repeated use they can help foster students' independence across a variety of writing. An added benefit is that they reduce teachers' grading load, and increase timely, focused, and actionable feedback. Schmoker (as cited in Collins, 2007) says the "research is strong that students are far better off when we score their work for only one or two criteria that we have just finished teaching carefully and explicitly" (p. vi).

While all learning outcomes don't necessarily call for students to write for an authentic audience, writing can still foster student engagement when tasks are complex and students have choice whether the writing is informational, narrative, argumentative, or analytical. When writing contests aren't an option, students also become very passionate when they collaborate and write to principals, the board of education, and various organizations to bring attention to issues they deem unfair. When students know their voices will be heard and their writing can effect change, they learn about the inimitable power of good writing.

My seventh-grade teacher helped me feel like I was worth something, and I was capable of accomplishing great things. After class, we used to talk about questions, news, or something I wanted to tell her. Above all, when I see her in eighth grade and now, she remembers who I am. I realized that by actively being part of a class, not only does the teacher impact you, you impact the teacher. —Ninth grader

---

Archetypal Character Exploration

During our study of Homer's (8th century BC/1999) *The Odyssey*, my students and I identify together how characters fit into archetypal models, and then we analyze how those characters break the archetypes and reveal their complexities. From there, students choose from a selection of short stories with clearly defined archetypal characters to further solidify their understanding. Their task is to identify the archetype, notice how the character breaks the mold, and explain how he or she emerges as a complex, dynamic character. Lastly, we compare this new understanding of archetypes to how people are also so much more than their stereotypes.

These conversations become a springboard to discussions about how we can try to further empathize and cultivate a deeper appreciation for the people around us. This culminates in a writing assignment in which students find a book, movie, television series, or real-life example that demonstrates an archetypal model that conveys the complexities of the human experience (figure 5.4).

Main Archetypes

Hero: Predominantly exhibits goodness and works against evil to restore harmony and justice to society

Mother: Guides and directs children; offers spiritual and emotional nourishment

Evil stepmother: Treats children unfairly; spiteful and jealous

The good wife: Devoted to and unquestionably supportive of her husband

Victim: The underdog, hurt by the villain; often takes the blame for everything bad that happens

Villain: Main function is to oppose the hero or who the hero must destroy to bring justice

Practice

Sample: *Archetype—the good wife. Appears in "Lamb to the Slaughter" by storyteller and author Roald Dahl (1953; https://bit.ly/1Ij7TVK).*

Questions to consider:

How does the wife fit the archetype of the good wife?

How does she break this archetypal mold?

How does this add to the complexity of the character?

How does this make the story more compelling for the reader?

How is the analysis of this character significant in the world beyond the story?

Application

Directions: Can you think of a person or a character from a fictional story, book, movie, television series, or in real life (media, popular culture, politics) that fits into one of the archetypal definitions? Check if your idea works by testing it with the same questions as in our practice example.

Questions to consider:

How does this person or character fit the archetypal model?

How does she or he break this archetypal mold?

How does this add to the complexity of the person or character?

Transfer: Archetype Writing Opportunity

Directions: Write an analytical response one-and-a-half to three pages long. Demonstrate your understanding of archetypal models. Determine what you want your reader to do, think, or feel as a result of your writing.

Questions to consider:

How does the person or character represent this archetype?

How is this person or character complex and resist the constraints of this archetypal definition?

What is the significance of the character's nuances and complexities, and how do these impact the character, plot, or theme? (If it's a real-life example, what are the circumstances surrounding the person?)

Why is this person or character worth consideration?

Role: Student writer seeking academic inquiry

Purpose: Share insights about the importance of understanding archetypes.

Audience: Teacher and academic community

Source: Adapted from Berit Gordon, literacy consultant, 2019.

Figure 5.4: Exploring archetypal characters.

Visit **go.SolutionTree.com/literacy** for a free reproducible version of this figure.

One fairly reticent student focused on how, in the movie *Man of Steel* (Roven, Nolan, Thomas, Snyder, & Snyder, 2013), Superman broke the archetype of the hero, but the student wasn't exactly sure how. She rewatched the film with a critical eye to notice the character's nuances, and when she arrived in class excited to report her findings, it gave me the chance to really get to know her and strengthen our connection. It was the best essay she wrote all year!

As archetypes are apparent throughout literature and life, teachers can adapt this analysis and writing opportunity to also include nonfiction texts and primary sources. This opportunity meets many common state standards that require students to understand explicit and implicit meanings, the people, characters, events, and themes over the course of a text, and write for different tasks, purposes, and audiences.

Metacognitive Writing

In her ninth-grade honors biology and twelfth-grade human anatomy and physiology courses, teacher Kate Heavers believes it is essential for each student to make meaning for him- or herself. As a dedicated, reflective teacher at West Windsor-Plainsboro High School South, Kate has thought a great deal about teacher-student relationships, classroom climate, and the power of listening. She has incorporated these beliefs into her teaching practice:

> What is it about *being listened to* that makes for such a feeling of safety and belonging? It's complicated, but we know that being listened to makes us feel as though we are being seen, and perhaps even being cherished. As a classroom teacher and authority in the room, when I stop speaking in order to listen intently to a student, I am saying, silently and implicitly, "You matter." This is the gift that listening gives. (K. Heavers, personal communication, May 17, 2019)

Kate's mission is for students to explore how they think, their actions, their study habits, how they feel during an assessment, and how they learn most effectively, with a focus on their process, not their results. She encourages self-reflection in her science students by incorporating structured time throughout the year and culminating in an end-of-year writing assignment. She adapted this idea from her colleague, Barbara Fortunato, who teaches advanced placement (AP) physics.

The day after an assessment, Kate returns a blank copy of each assessment to students. Students then go through the test in small groups and discuss each problem to reflect on how they did, what they struggled with, and what they still don't understand. She wants students to reflect on their performance the very next day so their feedback is immediate, deep, and actionable. The student feedback also provides Kate information about what she needs to reteach or clarify further. Following this group activity, students have thirty minutes to reflect using the handout in figure 5.5, which asks students to consider themselves learners in the context of Dweck's (2006, 2015) research on fixed and growth mindset.

Title of assessment: **Date of assessment:**
Scores of different components (multiple choice, short answer, and essay):
How did you prepare for this assessment?
If you met with the teacher for help in advance, what did you gain from the meeting? If you didn't gain anything, why not?
What did you do well on this assessment?
What mistakes did you make?
Was there anything you were confused about during the assessment but now understand?
What are the primary lessons you learned from this assessment, and what are you going to do differently next time?
According to Dweck's (2006, 2015) research, someone who has a *fixed mindset* thinks intelligence is automatically set. This can lead to only doing work that is easy, easily giving up on tough things, thinking there is no reason to try, and ignoring constructive feedback. People who have a *growth mindset* believe they can work on their intelligence. They take on challenges, keep trying even when they fail, think trying is worthwhile, and try to learn from constructive feedback.
Have you embraced a growth mindset? If so, how, when, and why? Be specific.
Everyone has both mindsets. Which mindset is your predominant one now, on this date, _______________? Explain why.
What have you learned about the way you learn and grow? What are you going to keep doing to continue to improve not just in this course but also in all of your studies and endeavors, both in and out of school?
What can I do to help you improve in this course? Be specific.

Source: ©2019 by Kate Heavers. Used with permission.

Figure 5.5: Student metacognitive log.

Visit **go.SolutionTree.com/literacy** for a free reproducible version of this figure.

By giving students time to self-reflect as learners in such a comprehensive manner, Kate implicitly sends the message that listening to themselves is valuable and necessary to advance as thinkers and learners. Kate strengthens relationships and further shows her students she values them by commenting on these student self-reflections throughout the year.

Students consider their own qualitative and quantitative data, along with Kate's comments from their ten months' worth of metacognitive notes, to write a five-page paper. She further requires students to incorporate excerpts from researchers Linda Darling-Hammond, Kim Austin, Melissa Cheung, and Daisy Martin's (n.d.) "Session 9: Thinking About Thinking—Metacognition" and connect them to their own findings (figure 5.6).

Step one: Read these excerpts from "Session 9: Thinking About Thinking—Metacognition" (Darling-Hammond et al., n.d.) in preparation for writing your paper.

"Sometimes people use the phrase 'going meta' when talking about metacognition, referring to the process of stepping back to see what you are doing, as if you were someone else observing it. 'Going meta' means becoming an audience for your own performance—in this case, your own intellectual performance. When a person is learning to play golf, for example, seeing a videotape of her own swing can help her to understand what she is doing well and what she is doing poorly. Typically, we do not know what we are doing when we do it, but it is very hard to improve a process that we are engaged in if we do not have a sense of what we are doing in the moment." (p. 158)

"Even a skilled professional ballet dancer relies on mirrors to help him understand what he looks like and what he is doing as he dances. He has to be able to see his performance as others might see it before he can begin to improve it. The ability to view our own performance is particularly useful when we learn physical skills. However, cognitive work is often invisible and cannot be directly observed." (p. 158)

John Dewey (1933), a progressive educator, said, "As long as our activity glides smoothly along from one thing to another . . . there is no call for reflection. Difficulty or obstruction in the way of reaching a belief brings us, however, to a pause. In the suspense of uncertainty, we metaphorically climb a tree; we try to find some standpoint from which we may survey additional facts and, getting a more commanding view of the situation, decide how the facts stand related to one another." (p. 14)

Step two: Read these excerpts about three kinds of metacognitive knowledge from psychologist John H. Flavell (1979).

"Awareness of knowledge—understanding what one knows, what one does not know, and what one wants to know. ('I know that I understand that plants need sunlight but I do not know why.') This category may also include an awareness of others' knowledge. ('I know that Sarah understands long division, so I'll ask her to explain this problem to me.')

"Awareness of thinking—understanding cognitive tasks and the nature of what is required to complete them. ('I know that reading this newspaper article will be easier for me than reading my textbook.')

"Awareness of thinking strategies—understanding approaches to directing learning." (p. 160)

Step three: Answer this question: Where were you in September 2018, and where are you now? Write a paper (at least five pages using twelve-point font, single spacing, one-inch margins on all four sides, numbered pages, and a title page—not included with the five pages—with a creative title and proper heading). Make it a metacognitive summary of your year in this course. You aren't limited to five pages, but that should be enough space.

Please address the ways you have grown intellectually, socially, and emotionally as a result of the coursework and pedagogical experiences of the past ten months. Use your metacognitive notes from your assessment portfolio to support your assertions. Remember these notes (and your scores) are the data, and your analysis will be your statements (grounded in the data) of the different ways you grew and developed.

Be sure to quote yourself and provide the date as an in-text citation. For example, if you quote yourself as having written "I stayed up so late studying for this test—I can't believe I didn't pass it" in October, include the month and year of the note following the statement. Later, you might quote yourself as having made a discovery: "After completing the two-week sleep journal, I realize that back in September I was studying more and sleeping less; now I sleep more and study less" (January 2019).

You may do outside research if you wish. If you do, please include a bibliography. If you don't, no bibliography is necessary.

Source: Adapted from Darling-Hammond et al., n.d. ©2019 by Kate Heavers. Used with permission.

Figure 5.6: Metacognition last paper directions.

Visit **go.SolutionTree.com/literacy** for a free reproducible version of this figure.

Kate further encourages students to put these reflections into the context of how they see themselves as learners by thinking about their lives as students across their school career as well as across the disciplines. This type of assignment aligns with many common state standards because it requires students to formulate their thinking through writing for a particular task, purpose, and audience in a clear and concise manner. Kate says these papers are enlightening because not only does she learn about her students' journeys as learners but also can use these reflections as feedback to improve her instruction.

While Students Are Working

Once students engage in a writing activity, the teacher should step back and support each student on their individual journey. Dewey's (1938) words relay that sentiment:

> A primary responsibility of educators is that they not only be aware of the general principle of the shaping of actual experience . . . but that they also recognize in the concrete what surroundings are conducive to having experiences that lead to growth. (p. 40)

While students are working, teachers can provide online resources (for example, articles and videos) via Google Classroom, with relevant handouts available in the classroom. Often, I remain available to all students with the open chair and an invitation (page 25), and if there is a backlog of students who want to talk to me, each writes his or her name on the board, and I call each in turn. Other times, I offer small-group instruction students can sign up for and participate in, and I circulate and observe which students need my support and determine how I can best help them.

My seventh-grade teacher allowed us to write stories in our notebooks about anything. She was super supportive of my writing, and that is what pushed me to actually publish one of the stories that I wrote.
—Ninth grader

On days when I think students need quiet time to work, their desks are set in rows. Some students use this time to enjoy the silence while others wear earbuds; the only voices in the room are those of the student who is talking with me. On other days, the classroom is buzzing. Students are asking one another questions and checking one another's work. As students are working on different topics, I often email students articles and resources specific to their topic. The students often generate ideas for additional resources that I add to Google Classroom. This responsiveness further shapes the lesson design; students offer resources and curate details. Student involvement in lesson design is particularly evident during editorial writing because it is so intellectually engaging and surfaces numerous multilayered issues many had never considered. It truly felt effortless for me to work alongside students rather than as the person in charge. Student questions led to me recall articles I had read months before. I received emails over the weekend from students excitedly sharing research they discovered. Every time the open chair next to my desk was empty, another student eagerly sat down. This is the learning environment I strive to create in my classroom—a place where we work together like a fine-tuned engine and the learning extends beyond the classroom, not because it's homework, but because it matters.

I like to introduce a new skill at a pivotal point to advance learning, rather than inundate students with everything they need to know at the beginning of an assignment. For example, during editorial writing, I introduce how to write a counterargument only after students complete their research, draft most of their editorial, and are confident they fully support their position. Only when they reach this point are students ready to fully contemplate the other side. At this pivotal point, a lesson on how to write a counterargument feels relevant, and students are more motivated to listen because it directly affects their ability to move forward. Similarly, during archetype writing, I withhold what I call the so what-who cares question until students have fully completed their analysis and are ready to think more expansively. Then I ask, "How is the character analysis significant in the world beyond the story?" As designers, teachers know they are going to ask these questions and can include them in lesson plans.

We gradually release them to students when they are ready. Front-loading all the discrete writing moves at the beginning of an assignment minimizes the complexity of each move but can also be more information than students can process. Releasing them gradually enables students to fully immerse themselves in each step, and we can follow their lead to determine when they are ready to think more broadly and deeply.

Toward the end of a writing assignment can be a useful time to focus on the writer's craft. Once students have their ideas down on paper, they are more open to taking a closer look at their word choices and enhancing the impact of their work. Close reading exercises on writing style support the work students do in writing, so they are clear on the cumulative impact of word choice on meaning.

Once students invest in their writing, I try to teach them how to elevate their writing style with engaging activities that resonate and immerse them, much like a type of music can convey an emotion. I offer the example of author and journalist Ta-Nehisi Coates (CBS Sunday Morning, 2017), who strives to write pieces that will "haunt" readers and stay with them long after they finish reading. Coates (CBS Sunday Morning, 2017) says he often listens to music as he writes so he can be inspired to find the right words to craft writing that resonates in the same way as a song. I suggest to students that if they concentrate on the music coming through their earbuds, they can turn up the volume on their writing.

Students can also explore the power of words by reading aloud sentences from their drafts and brainstorming with their peers using a Y-chart (figure 5.7, page 122) as they ask themselves questions like, "What does this idea look like, sound like, and feel like?" and "What words or images can I use to convey this feeling to others?" Students then consider incorporating words from their completed Y-chart to enhance their overall writing impact.

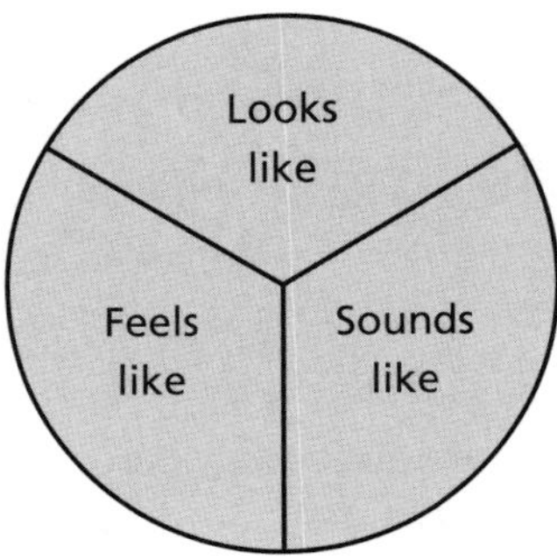

Figure 5.7: Y-chart to improve writing style.

Visit **go.SolutionTree.com/literacy** for a free reproducible version of this figure.

Feedback is how we learn and improve, and there is perhaps no place feedback is more essential than in writing. But feedback is criticism, and criticism hurts, especially when someone is criticizing a visual representation of our thoughts. Science author Angela Duckworth, in referencing how grit and growth mindsets can flourish in a classroom, says students "need to be able to say to themselves, 'I'm being challenged, I'm being asked to do something I can't yet do. But I can do it with some support and some practice and effort'" (as cited in McKibben, 2018). A classroom built on strong relationships and that fosters a sense of belonging provides the support students need to work alongside their teachers and listen to feedback about their writing and thinking—even when it's difficult to hear.

Our teacher this year helps us become better writers because he actually does it with us, and he goes through every one of our papers, comments, and fixes, to help! I found that really special, because going through twenty-four writing pieces is not easy. —Fifth grader

Since feedback is essential and grading writing is time consuming, teachers need to maximize opportunities for students to get more immediate feedback from peers, technology tools, and self-assessment as students measure their own performance against a rubric and other student work. Teachers may think students' peers are unable to provide meaningful feedback; however, the research indicates otherwise. Assessment expert and author Dylan Wiliam (2013) suggests "this is important because it suggests that with well-structured peer-assessment, one can achieve better outcomes than would be possible with one adult for every student" (p. 19).

Students often enjoy playing teacher and since student feedback isn't attached to grades, I encourage students to be honest with one another. I remind them it's kind to be accurate in your feedback because you are not only helping one another improve but also helping one another potentially earn higher grades. I think teachers need to carefully structure peer-editing time, so students make productive use of this time. Peer-editing time always looks different. Sometimes students are using highlighters and colored pencils, and other times they're commenting in Google Docs. I've created checklists with built-in accountability so students have to sign off on one another's work or submit evidence to me of their peer edits. I've had students grade one another on rubrics and grading sheets, and sometimes I require they submit these sheets with their final papers to receive credit. I often assign student pairs (either randomly or to complement students' strengths) to ensure there is more editing and less socializing. When students comment in Google Docs, they know their comments are visible to me, which also keeps them accountable.

I follow Wiggins's (2012) guidelines to ensure all feedback is designed to advance learning outcomes (figure 5.8).

Feedback Essentials	Description
Goal Referenced	"Effective feedback requires that a person has a goal, takes action to achieve the goal, and receives goal-related information about his or her actions."
Tangible and Transparent	"Any useful feedback system involves not only a clear goal, but also tangible results related to the goal."
Actionable	Effective feedback is concrete, specific, and useful; it provides actionable information.
User-Friendly	Offer "one important thing . . . that, if changed, will likely yield immediate and noticeable improvement."
Timely	Ensure students get more timely feedback and opportunities to apply the feedback shortly thereafter.
Ongoing	"Adjusting our performance depends on not only receiving feedback but also having opportunities to use it."
Consistent	Feedback must be "stable, accurate, and trustworthy," with shared exemplars.
Progress Toward a Goal	Improving performance requires adjusting according to "ongoing feedback that measures performance against a concrete, long-term goal."

Source: Wiggins, 2012.

Figure 5.8: Wiggins's keys to effective feedback.

It is essential that we give feedback tailored to each student's needs. A learner-centered classroom built on a strong foundation of relationships and belonging supports teachers' ability to personalize feedback so it can be heard and understood:

> Knowing the students allows the teacher to make better judgments about when to push each student and when to back off. Second, when students trust the teacher, they are more likely to accept the feedback and act on it. Ultimately, the only effective feedback is that which is acted upon, so that feedback should be more work for the recipient than the donor. (Wiliam, 2013, p. 18)

Remember the importance of mitigating the impact of grades as students work to improve their writing. The assessment's purpose is to determine if students have learned what the teacher intended, as well as to use these results to inform further instruction. However, it's important not to offer students a false sense of who they are as writers; they should always have clearly delineated performance standards to strive for. In my class, students track their progress and self-assess using our departmental rubric, and to also earn a grade. However, since many students don't quickly advance through the mastery of skills on this rubric, their writing grades hover in the same range, which can feel very disappointing. To create a balance, students receive another grade based on areas I emphasize during the lesson so all students can attain mastery. For example, consider the departmental rubric. Perhaps they can't write in a way that is insightful and comprehensive, but they can meet the focus correction areas that ask them to cite two direct quotations, write in a way that is honest and straightforward, and try to make readers care. Consequently, students earn two grades on their writing: one from the standardized rubric and the other using Collins's (2007) focus correction areas (figure 5.9).

The grade for the focus correction area lessens the impact of the departmental rubric grade, offers students an opportunity to be successful, and preserves an accurate picture of students' present writing ability as indicated on the departmental writing rubric.

Second Chances and Do-Overs

Offering students the opportunity to implement feedback and rewrite is how they grow as writers. Further, instilling confidence in students' ability to improve by suggesting they can do better by trying again is essential (Darga, 2017). After all, as my colleague Mark Wise writes, "school and life are about learning, not about getting it right the first time, or at the same time as other people" (Pandolpho & Wise, 2018).

- Letter clearly answers the prompt and demonstrates how the literary work impacted the letter writer. ____/10
- Letter includes at least two direct quotations from the text. ____/4
- Letter writer demonstrates time spent with his or her use of stylistically sophisticated writing (imagery, descriptive language, or compositional risks) and minimal grammatical errors. ____/2
- Writing is honest and straightforward. ____/2
- Readers should be able to see themselves in the writing or at least care about it, and the letter should have an emotional impact on the reader. ____/2

Source: Adapted from Collins, 2007.

Figure 5.9: Focus correction areas.

Visit **go.SolutionTree.com/literacy** for a free reproducible version of this figure.

Since the notion of having students rewrite and resubmit papers after the relief of grading and returning one-hundred-plus essays is understandably daunting, I create opportunities to demonstrate my belief that students can improve while also making assessment manageable for me. Sometimes, I offer an individual student the opportunity to rewrite if the student is particularly dejected about a grade or shows an overall lack of improvement over time. I target specific areas for improvement, provide feedback the student can act on, and then grade the revised work. Students' faces light up at this vote of confidence and chance for improvement. When offering an entire class a second chance, I may offer a targeted rewrite opportunity where students decide on one area to improve (figure 5.10, page 126) based on the feedback, thereby increasing their autonomy.

These papers are relatively quick to review. Teachers may choose to offer students points on their original paper if their rewrite is especially impressive, but I generally treat these types of revisions as separate, lower-stakes assignments.

I remind students that regardless of how well written a paper may be, if it doesn't achieve its desired effect, then it falls short of being a resounding success. I call this the writing's impact, and inform students after I read their papers if their writing had the desired impact. If it did not, I offer a redo opportunity. This doesn't generate a new paper that I need to grade, nor does it replace their writing grade. I make the determination based on the student and sometimes the number of students who require redos to maintain the integrity of students' grades and make the influx of redos manageable. I provide the rewrite opportunity in figure 5.11 (page 126) for editorials.

Directions

1. Read the comments.
2. Choose a few sentences that you may want to rewrite based on the feedback.
3. Before you decide which sentence to focus on, consider why these sentences need to improve.
4. Copy the original sentences here.
5. Write a revision of the sentences here.

Figure 5.10: Rewrite and revise.

Visit **go.SolutionTree.com/literacy** for a free reproducible version of this figure.

The purpose of these editorials was to convince the reader to agree with you. An editorial can be well written but not convincing. If your editorial was not convincing, it did not fulfill its primary purpose. Review your work with a fresh perspective and determine how you can improve it.

1. Read the feedback on your editorial. Choose a section to improve based on the feedback.
2. Copy the original text here.
3. Write the revised text here.

Figure 5.11: Editorial redo.

Visit **go.SolutionTree.com/literacy** for a free reproducible version of this figure.

Lastly, because the writing process can feel vast and mysterious, it is likely to generate many unanticipated student questions, responses, misunderstandings, and concerns. I've had students lament, "I always thought I was a pretty good writer until this year" or "I spent hours on this paper, and I don't understand why it still isn't very good" and the ever-popular, "I have no idea what to write about!" More confident writers ask questions like, "Can I write this assignment in verse?" or "Will I lose points if I exceed the word count?" Be prepared to make accommodations and adjustments to meet students wherever they happen to be on their journey as writers.

I assure students that it is well worth the time to carefully craft phrases that sing with meaning and unfold with grace, so their readers are more likely to understand, their parents are more likely to say yes, and their teacher is more likely to nod in agreement.

Questions for Reflection

Consider the following questions after reading the chapter.

How can I incorporate student choice and an authentic audience into the writing lessons already in my classroom?

What ideas from this chapter can I use to improve my practice?

What strategies from this chapter can I use to improve my practice?

What questions do I still have about teaching writing?

If you can't talk about something,
you can't think about something.
—Eula Biss

Developing Speakers and Listeners

Even more than reading and writing, we spend the majority of our lives speaking and listening. Yet, schools do not often focus on these skills. Speaking and listening skills tend to be difficult to assess and are rarely measured on standardized tests; teachers may question if their time is better spent focusing on the more measurable skills of reading and writing. However, the truth is both speaking and listening require a series of complicated processes that constitute many of the same critical-thinking skills reading and writing demand, and students need repeated practice in these areas to develop these essential skills.

When we speak, we process our thinking as we search for the exact words to convey our thoughts, read the social cues of our audience, and continually readjust our tone or approach as necessary to achieve our intention. When we listen, we simultaneously receive information, seek to understand it, assess what we hear, and then rely on our recall ability to decide how to react or respond. It challenges us because on hearing, we must "organize the information . . . understand its context or relevance, recognize unstated assumptions, make logical connections between ideas, determine the truth values, and draw conclusions" (Boundless.com, n.d). Unfortunately, the kinds of speaking and listening opportunities schools offer may not only feel contrived and disconnected from students' lives but also cannot necessarily demand the precise kind of practice students need.

We mustn't underestimate the value of listening; active listening requires critical thinking and listening that can expand our view of the world. Listening enables us to be the repository of the others' experiences while making them feel respected and cared for. Listening demonstrates we believe what people think matters and that they matter. Real, active listening can build relationships, and relationships are one of the essential components of living a happy and fulfilled life. Psychologist Esther Perel (2017) writes, "The quality of our relationships determines the quality of our lives."

Sharing stories, I learned firsthand, can be a bridge between strangers. I was one of ten teachers selected to tell a story at the final story slam at The Moth Teacher Institute in 2018. After speaking, a teacher came over and said my story reminded him of something that happened in his friend's family when he was growing up. He began pouring out the details of the story to me, and suddenly stopped and said he wasn't sure why he was telling me. Another teacher said, "I know this is an odd thing to say since I hardly know you, but I'm proud of you." It was easy to take in these shares and affirmations because I was similarly heartened and uplifted by many of the other storytellers. There was a lot of sincere hugging—the kind you give because there is nothing to say but you want to physically close the gap that existed before the story was told. And between classmates, sharing stories can build relationships.

If teachers align learning outcomes with what they want students to know and be able to do as speakers and listeners, along with what students want to become in their lives beyond school, teachers can design activities to lead them to these goals. Teachers want students to be active, informed, and empathic participants in their personal, academic, and civic lives. They want students to advocate for themselves and others and engage in academic discussions about books, ideas, and controversial issues. Students may not recognize these intricacies, but they do intuitively understand the importance of being competent, confident communicators. In her TED Talk, radio host Celeste Headlee (2015) asks, "Is there any 21st century skill more important than being able to sustain coherent, confident conversation?" She is, of course, right.

This chapter includes ideas and strategies for immediate use to build students' capacity for speaking to others (including in front of a larger audience), as well as actively listening across a variety of contexts. The chapter includes activities to strengthen students' ability to engage in worthwhile and sometimes controversial discussions independent of the teacher, and to share their ideas with conviction and clarity with a willingness to change based on what they hear. The chapter also includes strategies to incorporate oral storytelling and hone presentation skills.

Speaking and Listening in a Learner-Centered Classroom

There is a vast difference between who students are as speakers and as listeners. We each have our own particular affect, feelings, and dispositions. Author Elizabeth Gilbert (2006) illustrates this truth in her memoir *Eat, Pray, Love*, when she writes about how she sought to achieve silence and solitude during her visit to an ashram in India. She writes, "I decide that I've been talking too much. To be honest, I've been talking too much my whole life, but I've really been talking too much during my stay at the Ashram" (Gilbert, 2006, p. 189). She resolves to take a vow of silence.

My choir class has a project called Project Soul, where each kid talks about one thing that they are passionate about. Not only did it help me with public speaking and performing, but it also made me realize the things in my life that are going well that I should be grateful for. —Twelfth grader

And yet, hard as she tries, she can't escape her natural tendencies. Soon after, an Ashram staff member approaches Gilbert with her new work detail. It seems they need someone "social and bubbly and smiling all the time," and selected her (Gilbert, 2006, p. 203). She quickly understands that although she can make some personal improvements, she needs to truly accept herself to improve: "You make some big grandiose decision about what you need to do, or who you need to be, and then circumstances arise that immediately reveal to you how little you understood about yourself" (Gilbert, 2006, p. 191). Much in the same way, we need to honor our students' uniqueness and guide them as they set achievable goals for the speakers and listeners they hope to become.

Many students are reluctant to participate in whole-class discussions for fear of being wrong, and because they dread speaking aloud in class at all. Other students happily dominate the air time, so a whole-class discussion becomes a discussion between the teacher and the three most outgoing students. These same students relish any opportunity to get in front of the class, often unwittingly upstaging other members of the class.

I often remind students it is important to be an active participant in class because the one who is doing the talking is doing the learning. Schmoker (2006) writes, "Discussion—talk about books and other texts—is where students develop . . . an appreciation for the power of ideas, including their own" (p. 70). According to English professor Gerald Graff (2003), "Good talk—about books and subjects—stimulates the intellect and is the enemy of boredom. . . . It nourishes our critical capacities as it gives kids a chance to try on and test their ideas and viewpoints" (p. 3).

Before students begin to practice their speaking and listening skills, our classroom has to offer continued opportunities for students to understand who they are as speakers and listeners. Students who tend to talk must recognize themselves as those who need to listen more intentionally, and quieter students need to devise strategies to find openings to add to the conversation. Students' understanding that they are welcomed and accepted in our classroom supports them in their quest to find their unique starting point. Speaking and listening skills development, no matter how low stakes, still requires a very public display in front of their peers.

To Begin

If students don't value what we teach them, it is unlikely they will engage with learning opportunities. Relevance matters to engagement, so teachers should share why developing speaking and listening skills matters. Both skills require active participation, and there are very real strategies for doing each of these well. Whether it's with more outgoing students or more reticent students, there is progress to be made in speaking with intention and quieting down long enough to hear others. Headlee (2015) says, "You need to enter every conversation assuming you have something to learn."

Designing learning opportunities with the end in mind ensures listening is an equal priority. Teachers often provide students with many opportunities to speak in school—they can work with partners, engage in small-group discussions, participate in larger-group discussions, and give presentations. It is not enough for teachers to prioritize listening by insisting everyone face the student speaking and nod at appropriate intervals. We need to give students a purpose for listening. What do we expect students to do with the shared information? How do we incentivize listening?

By design, all speaking activities should also emphasize and incentivize listening. If teachers create an environment where students understand the value of listening and gain something doing so, listening becomes a natural outgrowth. Engaging experiences that pique students' curiosity will get them listening and learning from one another. In addition, if teachers offer specific strategies, repeated speaking practice, and meaningful speaking opportunities, students' peers will have something worth listening to—listening becomes more than an act of compliance. In his TED Talk, Julian Treasure (2013) offers guidelines for not only what to say, but how to say it. To increase the likelihood that people will listen to you, Treasure (2013) advocates speaking honestly, being yourself, "standing in your truth," and having good will toward your listeners; he also reminds us that it is not only what we say, but how we say it—speed, volume, pitch, and even the rhythm.

My current health class has helped me because we talk about mental health and our personal lives. It's like free therapy. —Twelfth grader

As the steward charting this course, the teacher's modeling of good listening is crucial. When students are faced with a supportive class that listens and a compassionate teacher who won't let them suffer through a presentation clearly causing them distress, it encourages students to take speaking and listening risks and ultimately, encourages progress. West Windsor-Plainsboro High School South science teacher Kate Heavers uses what she and her students refer to as *the bell* in student-led speaking and listening activities in order to empower her students to sustain their own discussions: "It is a brass bell that once belonged to our high school's first head custodian from 1971 to 1996. For me, it is a daily reminder of how much he loved our school and the people in it" (K. Heavers, personal communication, May 17, 2019).

During whole-class student-led discussions, Kate assigns a student the job of ringing the bell the moment the student hears her voice. Kate wants the class to forget that she's even there and to do the thinking and learning on their own. Kate further explains, "When I interrupt their sacred student-only space because I just cannot help myself, the student with the bell rings it vigorously and generally everyone laughs as I remember to be quiet and listen." Kate's students are well prepared prior to any student-led discussion, and she conveys her trust in them by staying silent and listening. Kate says, "Trusting students makes them feel powerful. Even when I hear a student say something wrong, I'll often wait to give the students time to correct one another before stepping in. If it becomes time to intervene, I'll ask the student with the bell, 'Permission to speak?'" (K. Heavers, personal communication, May 17, 2019).

Teachers must be mindful of the pressure contrived presentations and other speaking opportunities can put on students. As Chapman University's (2018) study about fears reveals, public speaking, without fail, always makes the list. A trembling student who can't utter a word should be met with the snapping of supportive fingers, and an offer to perhaps try again when he or she feels ready. A visibly nervous student who needs more time should have the opportunity to indicate with a gesture to the teacher that he or she needs more time, and should feel confident the teacher will tacitly understand the gesture and respond accordingly.

Since each student needs to decide how to improve his or her own speaking and listening skills, at the beginning of the year I offer students the opportunity to set their own speaking and listening goals (figure 6.1, page 134). I pose the question, "Who do you want to be as a speaker and a listener?"

Directions: Choose **one speaking goal** and **one listening goal** in an area you'd like to improve. We will revisit and reflect on these throughout the school year. If you have an idea not shown here, you can design your own goal or we can create one together.

Civility

Speaking

Use sensitivity to take turns.

Speak to classmates, as well as to the teacher, and align my body to make eye contact with other students.

Listening

Listen with the intent to learn something new instead of to react or respond.

Use sensitivity to not interrupt others and wait before adding my own ideas, ensuring the speaker has completed his or her thoughts.

Listen to classmates as well as to the teacher; look at the speaking student and give nonverbal cues that I am paying attention.

Connection Making

Speaking

Relate prior knowledge (both academic and personal) to the topic of discussion.

Offer reasons and textual evidence to support my point of view.

Listening

Respond with similarities and differences between my ideas and those of others.

Offer reasons and textual evidence to support other students' points of view.

Questioning

Speaking

Begin speaking with a question, rather than a comment, to deepen inquiry.

Listening

Pose questions to clarify or anticipate the thinking or reasoning behind a speaker's argument or conclusion, or ask *what-if* questions to encourage divergent thinking.

Expanding

Speaking

Piggyback to elaborate on classmates' comments.

State inferences from different speakers' ideas to take the conversation deeper.

Listening

Integrate information from multiple sources to produce a new way of thinking.

Figure 6.1: Sample speaking and listening goals.

Visit **go.SolutionTree.com/literacy** for a free reproducible version of this figure.

Students add these self-selected goals to their Quotes of the Week document or the front of their writer's notebooks so they see them every day. As we participate in speaking and listening activities, I cue students to revisit their goals, set an intention, establish a plan of action to meet these goals, and continually reflect on their progress. To emphasize the importance of these goals, I offer low-stakes speaking and listening opportunities throughout the year without the pressure of a grade, but with time for self-assessment and specific feedback about what students did well and how to improve both their speaking and listening skills.

Speaking

When it comes to speaking skills, I remind my students there are more purposeful ways of talking that enable others to really hear what we have to say, and that if they follow my lead, I will show them how. I often give students time (even briefly) to write first and encourage sharing aloud. I allow my uneasy students to share by reading verbatim what they write. To me, this is an opening to increase their comfort with participation over the course of the school year. Early in the year, I assure students I'll never cold-call on them, but I do create moments when I give everyone adequate time to prepare and tell them to be ready because everyone should have an answer when I call a name.

My second-grade teacher gave everyone cute nicknames. Although this might sound silly, it really made me feel wanted and helped me get to know everyone. I started talking in class more often and became a much more confident speaker. Every Friday, we would just relax and talk about everything. She worked really hard to make sure that every single one of us felt important and that everyone was included. —Ninth grader

---

To encourage students to participate as well as bounce questions around or expand on others' comments, I project sentence and question stems to prompt discussion on the SMART Board in a large font for easy reference (figure 6.2, page 136). I quietly alert students I'd most like to hear from and offer a wait time before calling on them. All of this seems contrived, but it works quite naturally. These structures help students gather and frame their thoughts in order for others to understand. It also helps them feel less worried about making a mistake because the stems literally support their response. Over time, these scaffolded, low-stakes opportunities pave the way for increased, easier participation. Certainly, students remain true to their nature, but this is a path to clear progress.

Sentence Stems to Begin	Phrases and Questions to Encourage Listening and Continue Conversation
• "I noticed how . . ." • "I liked (didn't like) . . . because . . ." • "I don't understand . . ." • "I am wondering . . ." • "I agree (disagree) because . . ." • "I think that maybe . . ."	• "I heard you say . . ." • "I'm also wondering . . ." • "Can you tell me more about why you think . . .?" • "Can you explain . . .?" • "What did you mean by . . .?" • "In what ways do you think . . .?"

Figure 6.2: Student-sustained conversation ideas.

Visit **go.SolutionTree.com/literacy** for a free reproducible version of this figure.

Listening

To encourage students to even consider listening a skill worth attending to, I remind them listening offers them the opportunity to become the repository of others' experiences. I describe how we all have endless room for expansion in our minds and hearts, and listening is one way to grow. However, active listening is more than standing in a room and looking at the person who is talking. According to Maria Popova, founder of Brain Pickings (https://brainpickings.org):

> We never see the world exactly as it is because we are how the world is . . . In choosing how we are in the world, we shape our experience of that world, our contribution to it. We shape our world, our inner world, our outer world, which is really the only one we'll ever know. (as cited in Tippett, 2019b)

From this quotation, we can infer by listening; we not only create what we know but also become who we are. As listeners, we learn different perspectives, challenge our own beliefs, and actually become more interesting people as we think critically about the ideas and experiences we learn through listening. Also, "empathic listening has been hailed as a core component of competent communication, primarily because it has been linked to many positive listener outcomes" including "more satisfying friendships and . . . better understanding" (Allen, 2017). The research clearly points to the fact that listening well, in addition to leading us to greater understanding, is one of the ways to build lasting relationships. In other words, "if social relationships are vital for a happy and fulfilling life, and a vital element of social interaction is good conversation, then we are lost without the skills of active listening" (Ohlin, 2019). If we want to realize these benefits, we need to practice. Listening is an active process composed of strategies that extend far beyond eye contact and head nodding. As listeners, we need to pay attention to the speaker, ask questions, occasionally paraphrase the speaker to ensure our understanding, and resist the urge to fill pauses and brief moments of silence.

I extend this idea by asking students how they feel when people listen to them. Together, we discover that by listening, we show others we care about them. People generally like to talk about themselves, and they like the people who listen to them. When we listen and show interest in other people, we create a stronger social network.

The benefit to identifying these behaviors early in the year is so teachers can easily cue students throughout the year when they notice students are not listening. Since students tend to associate listening with quiet compliance, early in the school year I delve into the specifics of the skill. I draw a Y-chart on the board (like that in figure 5.7, page 122) and ask student groups to brainstorm responses to the question, What does listening look like, sound like, and feel like?

Sometimes when you begin with identifying the moves, the actions naturally follow. Then, I issue some quick reminders: "I'm not seeing good listening" along with descriptors, or "Laptops should be closed, and I don't see everyone facing the student who is talking." Again, just because students look like they're listening doesn't mean they are, but often teacher corrections bring them into the mindset to begin listening. This gentle insistence on listening reinforces the fabric of a supportive classroom culture and how to treat one another.

Since learning doesn't necessitate a grade, teachers do not have to assess every learning opportunity. Surprisingly, this truth is often news to students. Sometimes, students offer brief remarks in the front of the room, then everyone watches and listens and reflects on how they did. Because suspending judgment is one of the keys of active listening, resisting the urge to assign a grade implicitly models good listening (Ohlin, 2019).

Speaking and Listening Activities

The common thread between these activities is they encourage students to speak and listen in ways that either imitate real-world experiences or offer practice settings to help students transfer these skills to the world beyond the classroom.

The following activities offer a variety of speaking opportunities that incentivize listening while also strengthening relationships and enhancing belonging.

My social studies teacher always tells us to voice our opinion and that our opinion matters, which makes me more confident and really motivates me on the inside. —Seventh grader

Low-Stakes Speaking Opportunities

Our classroom culture supports low-stakes speaking opportunities because they communicate and reinforce the tacit understanding that our primary focus is on learning and personal growth. Students are already immersed in a culture where their parents, teacher, and peers measure and judge them, so remind them they matter and we, as a class, can focus on learning.

Quote Share

Quote sharing works well, especially at the beginning of the school year. This activity offers students an opportunity to increase their comfort level for speaking at the front of the room by sharing a quote from a book they are reading (or read over the summer) that resonates with them. An easy way to accomplish this is to create an editable Google Slides presentation and assign each student a number. Students type their chosen quote in a large font on the corresponding slide, and perhaps add a visual for interest. Teachers can offer students the opportunity to customize the font and color, too.

Students come up to the front of the room and the teacher sits in the back, ensuring the quote is displayed next to the student. Teachers can have students share why the quote means something to them or just listen to the author's words and move quickly through each slide. Students walk up in numerical order, share their quotes, and then return to their seats.

To extend this activity, you can share the file after the presentations are complete, so students can review the quotes meaningful to them and respond to them in a reflective writing opportunity. For a less formal reflection, students share their thoughts about how comfortable (or uncomfortable) they are presenting in front of the room and address these questions in small groups.

- What was the hardest part? The easiest part?
- What were you most worried about?
- What would you like to do better next time?

Of course, well-selected quotes in and of themselves are thought provoking and therefore incentivize listening, but it helps if students know they are accountable for reflecting on these quotes. Sharing the quote file promotes conversation and personal connection, so this activity quite naturally strengthens relationships and further builds classroom culture.

Iambic Pentameter Beat

Kwame Ivery, young adult author and English teacher at Collingswood High School in New Jersey, offers a novel approach to student presentations when he teaches about the works of Shakespeare (K. Ivery, personal communication, February 16, 2019). It is a bit of a departure from what students have come to expect at school. His students write poems (figure 6.3).

Write a poem about anything you want, but you must follow these rules.

- It must contain six lines total.
- It can be in blank verse, which means it doesn't have to rhyme.
- Each line must be in iambic pentameter, which means each line should have ten or eleven syllables—not more, not less.
- You will take turns going to the front of the room and reading your poems to the class.

The following poem is an example of what I'm looking for.

That crazy girl just took all my money.

I can't believe I thought she was my honey.

After all these years of building up trust,

Her love for me has legit turned to dust.

So, to keep your heart from falling on the shelf,

The only person you should trust is yourself.

Source: ©2019 by Kwame Ivery. Used with permission.

Figure 6.3: Writing a poem in iambic pentameter.

Kwame says, "I wanted to give kids a taste of what Shakespeare went through whenever he sat down to write a play. When they turned in the assignment, I told them 'If you thought it was hard to write a six-line poem in iambic pentameter, imagine how hard it was for Shakespeare to sit down and write a one-hundred-page play where 90 percent of the dialogue was in iambic pentameter!'"

For their presentations, students read their poem aloud without the iambic-pentameter rhythm. Then, each student gets the choice to either reread the first line or the entire poem to the iambic-pentameter rhythm; the class provides the beat by banging on their desks. If a student is uncomfortable reading to the beat, Kwame steps in and reads for them. He managed to create a speaking opportunity that joins rhythm and poetry with students banging on desks in unison with vigor.

Viewing the TED-Ed video "Why Shakespeare Loved Iambic Pentameter" (https://bit.ly/35yi8GU) is a great way to teach students about the structure, and teachers can offer them familiar examples from Shakespeare's plays. Students also love hearing about the reason Shakespeare supposedly used iambic pentameter—not only to aid in memorization for the actors but also to mimic the sound of a heart beating, especially for when characters are confessing their love for one another (Freeman & Taylor, n.d.).

An honest sharing with a class of students tapping along in time to the beat can be a unifying experience and foster the sense of belonging teachers are striving to create in classrooms. Brown (2017) describes the joy and transcendence people feel when attending a concert together or collectively grieving in response to a national tragedy. Researchers Shira Gabriel, Jennifer Valenti, Kristin Naragon-Gainey, and Ariana F. Young (2017) use the term *collective assembly* to describe these types of experiences that "contribute to a life filled with 'a sense of meaning, increased positive affect, an increased sense of social connections, and a decreased sense of loneliness—all essential components of a healthy, happy life'" (as cited in Brown, 2017, p. 130). This activity also meets many state standards because it provides students with a speaking opportunity and requires that students analyze and implement a writer's craft to compose an original narrative poem.

Speed Dating

This activity is common in world language classes. It requires little preparation, and students really enjoy it. The Speed Dating activity offers students the opportunity to interact in a one-to-one setting (but with multiple peers), making students less self-conscious because they only speak to one peer at a time (versus the whole class at once), and get up and move around. Speed Dating works well in the following scenarios.

- You want students to share something specific, such as an artifact from their research project or a quick pitch of a novel they're reading.
- You want students to speak on a certain topic or in response to particular questions.
- Students are working on different projects or reading different books.

Even with the most unconventional activity, I like things tightly organized with a clear focus on learning outcomes. That structure provides students the support they need to engage freely in the activity. I explain the focus of the conversation and time each interaction, and I generally follow this format.

1. Students arrange their desks in a line facing one another and take a seat.
2. The speaker gets ninety seconds to talk uninterrupted.
3. The listener then gets the opportunity to ask the speaker one probing question.
4. The speaker has thirty seconds to respond.
5. The listener has thirty seconds to write down the main idea, or gist, of what the speaker shares.
6. Now the listener becomes the speaker. Repeat steps one through five.
7. For the next round, one row of students shifts over one seat and repeats the process with a new partner.
8. After speaking with each person, students record each person's name and the gist of what the listeners hear on a form I provide. (Visit **go.SolutionTree.com/literacy** for a free reproducible version of the form.)

As certain classes tend to be more talkative than others, I adjust these times accordingly based on whether students are still chatting or if the room falls silent. Before students switch partners, I have students write down the gist of what the speaker says to encourage listening. These one-to-one interactions often pair students with other students they've never spoken to individually. Speed dating builds a familiarity between students and eases the path for them to feel increasingly comfortable working with each of their classmates.

All of these low-risk speaking opportunities not only strengthen classroom culture but also meet many state standards which require students to participate in different types of collaborative discussions on relevant topics, clearly express their own ideas, and build on the ideas of their peers. After these activities, I often direct students to return to their speaking and listening goal sheets and assess their progress and comfort level, as well as consider steps to move closer to their personalized speaking and listening goal. Teachers can strengthen students' sense of belonging by reminding them that it doesn't matter so much where they stand on the continuum, as long as they're becoming better versions of themselves.

Student-Led Discussions

Teachers can build on students' progress from lower-stakes opportunities by creating deeper skill-building opportunities. One important skill is engaging in discussions without the presence of the teacher as facilitator. These discussions, regardless of content, prepare students to engage in civil dialogue throughout their personal and academic lives, and eventually, as active and informed citizens.

If teachers want to continually remove themselves from these student conversations to build independence, teachers must offer students conversations about worthwhile and consequential topics and issues with scaffolded conversational moves to help them sustain the conversations. This type of discussion aligns with many state standards because it requires that students participate in a discussion in which they draw on their knowledge to exchange ideas, challenge assumptions, and draw their own conclusions. A student-led discussion in a learner-centered classroom can only occur with a great deal of the teacher's behind-the-scenes planning. An uninformed observer might assume he or she is watching an advanced class or an unusually talkative and high-performing group, yet a well-run student-led discussion is a prime example of how a teacher's part of the design makes all the parts work.

Interdisciplinary

Teachers need to first decide why they want students to engage in a particular discussion, and what learning outcomes they hope students achieve. Maybe teachers want students to engage with the course content in specific ways, argue different sides of an issue, reference the text to support viewpoints, or actively listen to and build on one another's ideas. Once teachers decide on their intentions, they can plan the student discussion with purpose.

One example of a student-led discussion in Kate Heavers's class is when students discuss what their responsibility is in a country where people who are against vaccinating their children are gaining ground and compromising herd immunity. Students understand herd immunity is a public responsibility, and that 95 percent herd immunity can help prevent an outbreak, and yet people have begun to value the experience of the individual over communities (Pemberton, 2014). Students prepare in advance for this discussion by watching the PBS documentary film *Vaccines—Calling the Shots* (Pemberton, 2014; https://to.pbs.org/2kVgJJm). Students use information gleaned from the film and frame their discussion with focus questions like the following.

- How do we protect the immuno-compromised in a world where some people are deciding not to vaccinate their children?
- What do we do in a world where people value the individual over the collective good?
- Why are people so distrustful of science?
- What are you going to say to mothers on the playground who are confident in their decision not to vaccinate their children?

Prior to students entering any student-led, inquiry-based discussion, they should know key scientific principles, effective discussion techniques, and how to frame an argument and support it with evidence. Students must also be aware that when addressing opposing viewpoints, insults and negativity are not going to help change anyone's mind. Students must know to speak with genuine respect and concern for others to really hear them.

Kate teaches her students to be skeptical, and to think about what they trust and why. They understand people will listen to emotionally charged views if scientific data back them, and one data point can cause mass hysteria, as it did in the case of Andrew Wakefield and colleagues' 1998 study indicating vaccines cause autism (which the science research journal *Lancet* later retracted). At the conclusion of this discussion, students reflect on their own experience and opinions, and they write a response to this question: If you have children of your own one day, do you plan on vaccinating them, and why?

Students should always arrive prepared for a discussion with annotated texts and notes in which they've contemplated responses to the discussion questions. When I distribute the discussion questions, I briefly model how I might approach these questions using another text everyone is familiar with but is not a part of the upcoming discussion. Then I give students time to begin working in class so they can ask any questions. By the end of this class, they are fully equipped to prepare for the seminar independently at home (figure 6.4).

Texts

"To My Dear and Loving Husband" by Anne Bradstreet (n.d.)	*Common Sense and Other Writings* by Thomas Paine (1776/2003)	*Poor Richard's Almanac* by Benjamin Franklin (1849)	*Project for Moral Perfection* by Benjamin Franklin (1791/n.d.)
"Huswifery" by Edward Taylor (n.d.)	*The Crucible* by Arthur Miller (1953/1976)	"A Witch Trial at Mount Holly" by Benjamin Franklin (1730)	One text of your choice connected by topic or theme (annotated)

Directions: Prepare answers for each of the questions prior to the discussion using textual evidence from at least two of the preceding texts to support your responses. Bring your additional annotated source to the discussion as well.

Questions

- How do unrealistic expectations set people up for failure? Can you find textual evidence showing this failure with the Puritans and also Franklin? Can you find an example of this in today's society?

Continued ▶

Figure 6.4: Student-led discussion questions.

- How does hysteria spread among people, and in what ways are we still seeing this happen today? What are the consequences of hysteria, and how do we stop it?
- How was the Age of Reason a reaction to Puritanism, and what was the subsequent movement and how was it a reaction to the Age of Reason? Are we still reacting to former historical movements today?
- In what ways were some of the philosophies espoused during the Age of Reason similarly faulty to those of the colonial period? In what ways is it evident in American culture and today's society that we have our own questionable philosophies and haven't learned important lessons from the past?

The work across the disciplines may seem so different, but basic principles are very much in alignment. Both this science-based and language arts discussion enable students to apply their prior knowledge, engage in authentic discussion, practice real-life skills, and consider how the content of this discussion applies to their life outside the classroom. Teachers can reinforce these important skills across disciplines.

Open-Ended Questions

To stimulate a thoughtful and complex discussion, offer open-ended questions that inspire curiosity, drive conversation, teach students how to formulate their own questions, meet objectives, and align with course content. According to teacher and author Shanna Peeples (as cited in Ferlazzo, 2018):

> The fastest way to engage anyone's brain is to ask it [*sic*] a question. . . . As teachers, we can use this information as a sort of neurological hack. If we carefully scaffold students' questions in a way that points toward the content we need to teach, we can enlist their natural tendency to find answers into deeper learning experiences. These experiences then in turn develop their vocabulary, their speaking and listening skills, writing skills, their reading, and their critical thinking.

When organizing a student-led discussion, it is important to teach students how to generate questions as well as offer students questions that meet the guidelines of McTighe and Wiggins's (2013) essential questions coupled with a rich, complex text to anchor the conversation:

1. Is *open-ended*; that is, it typically will not have a single, final, and correct answer.
2. Is *thought-provoking* and *intellectually engaging*, often sparking discussion and debate.
3. Calls for *higher-order thinking*, such as analysis, inference, evaluation, prediction. It cannot be effectively answered by recall alone.

4. Points toward *important, transferable ideas* within (and sometimes across) disciplines.
5. Raises *additional questions* and sparks further inquiry.
6. Requires *support* and *justification*, not just an answer.
7. *Recurs* over time; that is, the question can and should be revisited again and again. (p. 3)

Teachers can powerfully drive the conversation by giving students time alone to refamiliarize themselves with their thoughts and prepared notes upon their arrival. This time can build students' confidence and prime them for conversation. Teachers may not think about it, but offering students time for quiet introspection conveys that teachers value the thoughts students have brought with them, and understand students' need to transition and reacquaint themselves with the text. This also shows students respect and reinforces the positive class culture.

Another way to enrich and add nuance to the conversation is to require that students bring in an ancillary reading connected to the text by topic or theme, and to consider in advance how this additional text is relevant to the discussion. The practice of students bringing in a supplemental text, coupled with open-ended questions, offers students some ownership and flexibility in determining what issues or problems they specifically want to interrogate. In other words, just as in the real world, valuable conversations occur when participants have a desire to prove their point, a curiosity about what others are thinking, and perhaps a few perplexing questions for which they'd like some answers.

The added value of carefully designing essential questions for student-led discussions is that a well-designed question aids in teaching for transfer, which helps students learn how to apply the skills they learn in school to their lives outside school. McTighe and Wiggins (2013) write:

> The important point is that the best essential questions are those that become the students' questions over time. The best questions evolve from being one that a teacher asks to one that thoughtful people consider on their own. . . [and because] these questions usefully recur over time; they never become moot or easily answered with finality. Indeed, answers may well evolve over a lifetime. (pp. 54–55)

I try to use essential questions that transcend units, so my students and I can revisit them throughout the school year. Eventually, I notice my students begin independently asking these same questions in class (and, I expect, beyond the class). This is teaching for transfer.

- What makes a great story? (McTighe & Wiggins, 2013)
- What truths have you uncovered from fiction?

- What connections can you make to other things you know, learned, or are studying?
- How does listening to others' perspectives enhance your view of yourself and the world?
- How important is education to a well-lived life?
- How does this issue relate to our lives? Why does it matter?

Discussion Norms and Conversational Moves

To further build students' capacity for independence, teachers should offer norms to regulate student-led discussions (Northwest Association for Biomedical Research, n.d., p. 108).

- Listen to learn, not simply to react or respond.
- Address one another respectfully.
- Base your opinions and comments on facts and textual evidence.
- "Address comments to the group."
- Have no side conversations.
- "Take turns and do not interrupt others."
- "Monitor 'air time.'"
- "Be courageous in presenting your own thoughts and reasoning."
- "Be flexible and willing to change your mind in the face of new and compelling evidence."

We also can offer the following conversational moves (which align with each speaking and listening goal; figure 6.5) for students to use to develop and organize their thoughts. Providing students with conversational moves during a discussion is similar to the writing templates offered for argumentative essays. Graff and Birkenstein (2010) find offering students some of the "language and patterns" improves "their quality of thought" (p. xviii).

Graff (2003) writes about how argument literacy is pivotal to a person's education because it grants "access to forms of intellectual capital that have a lot of power in the world" (p. 9). Offering students issues worthy of argument not only leads to spirited conversations but also the kinds of conversations they need to have in school. If teachers connect these worthy issues to why they matter in the real world and signal to students how they can apply these conversational skills to effect realities, teachers can explicitly teach students how to transfer essential speaking and listening skills to their lives outside school.

Speaking and Listening Goal Category	Student Conversational Moves
Civility	• Offer wait time to ensure the speaking student is finished. • Move your body and your eyes toward class members when you're speaking and toward the speaker when you're listening. • Preface your statements with phrases like these. ○ "I hear that you said . . . and I'm thinking . . . " ○ "I also noticed (or thought or wondered). . . "
Connection Making	• Preface your statements with phrases like these. ○ "That also reminds me of . . . " ○ "This relates (connects) to . . . " ○ "An example that supports your point of view is . . . "
Questioning	• Preface your statements with phrases like these. ○ "I am wondering if you also considered . . . ?" ○ "Why did you think . . . ?" ○ "Why does . . . ?" ○ "In what ways . . . ?" ○ "What do you mean . . . ?" ○ "Can you explain . . . ?" ○ "What if . . . ?"
Expanding	• Preface your statements with phrases like these. ○ "To expand on your point, . . . " ○ "If we combine the ideas, . . . " ○ "If we consider [student's] point along with [other student's] point, . . . " ○ "If we reframe the idea that . . . " ○ "If we re-envision the notion that . . . , we can infer . . . " ○ "How is . . . the same (different) than . . . ?" ○ "How would . . . change if this happened or didn't happen?" ○ "If all of this is true, what predictions can we make?"

Figure 6.5: Student conversational moves.

Visit **go.SolutionTree.com/literacy** for a free reproducible version of this figure.

One goal when helping students engage in dialogue and debate is to teach them to not focus solely on advancing their opinion, but to listen with curiosity and a willingness to adjust or expand their notion of what is right. In order for a student to really broaden his or her understanding or make a meaningful shift in opinion, he or she must acknowledge and accept part of the argument of the other side. Frances Kissling (as cited in Tippett, 2018b), president of the Center for Health, Ethics and Social Policy, offers two interesting questions to pose either before or after a controversial discussion:

- "What is it in your own position that gives you trouble?"
- "What is it in the position of the other that you are attracted to?"

If teachers ask these questions beforehand, they should also ask students to predict the opposing viewpoints they're likely to hear. By doing so, teachers are essentially helping students create a schema to enter a new conversation much the same way we all activate prior knowledge before beginning reading a new book. The opportunity to ponder these questions in advance creates a schema for listening and possibly tempers their impulse to reactively respond. If teachers offer these questions after a discussion, students can consider them in their reflection to offer them a deeper, more nuanced understanding of a controversial issue.

Overall, engaging in these types of discussions requires that students feel safe enough to be vulnerable and share an unpopular opinion, and have an openness to change based on what they hear. A classroom with strong relationships, mutual respect, and a sense of belonging enables students to confidently participate in this kind of discourse with the compassion and honesty required to improve speaking and listening skills. These discussions offer students the opportunity to consider multiple perspectives, develop empathy, understand the content more deeply, and strengthen their own ideological and social identity in the process. These student-led discussions align with many state standards because they require students to draw on their knowledge to exchange ideas, challenge assumptions, and draw their own conclusions.

Narrative Storytelling

The art of storytelling is another very different mode of helping students develop as speakers and listeners and achieve many of these same learning outcomes. Storytelling elements can be interwoven to reinforce the fabric of the classroom culture, as stories build community and stories build empathy. We can connect with one another through the stories we tell, and the classroom becomes a sanctuary for stories as they bind and support teachers and students through the work they do together. Stories are evidence of how different we are, while at the same time, so similar and worthy of belonging. Scientific research (Zak, 2014) proves that character-driven stories that elicit a strong emotional response actually bring people closer together, which further strengthens student connections.

Encourage students to tell their stories by continually reminding them when they read and listen to stories, it can be a gift to other people. Students are easily swayed to love fictional characters like Gerald and Piggie from Mo Willems's (2007) books, Opal from *Because of Winn-Dixie* (DiCamillo, 2000), Sodapop and Johnny from *The Outsiders* (Hinton, 1967), and Harry Potter and Hermione Granger from J.K. Rowling's (1997–2007) *Harry Potter* series as if they are best friends. Many of my students feel endless gratitude for slam poets like Sarah Kay and Shane Koyczan and comedian Hasan Minhaj for telling their stories, and in the process making them feel less alone and a bit better about themselves.

When teachers guide and encourage students to tell their stories in a way other people can really hear them, it begins to empower them to own their story. Writer and lecturer Andrew Solomon (2014) illustrates this truth in his TED Talk, "How the Worst Moments in Our Lives Make Us Who We Are." Solomon (2014) says he survived his childhood through a mixture of "avoidance and endurance." In the process, he learned "You need to take the traumas and make them part of who you've come to be, and you need to fold the worst events of your life into a narrative of triumph." Although Solomon's (2014) struggles may be different than our own, we can derive strength when we learn about how he and others have not only persevered through challenges but also managed to create meaning from the struggle.

Another integral part of students owning their own story is that it can help them feel less ashamed. Solomon (2014) says, "When we're ashamed, we can't tell our stories, and stories are the foundation of identity. Forge meaning, build identity." Perhaps one of the best gifts teachers can offer students is to help them forge meaning from their struggles and strengthen their identities through storytelling while developing their speaking skills. Micaela Blei, former director of education at The Moth (https://themoth.org), a nonprofit group based in New York City dedicated to the art and craft of storytelling, says, "We don't just tell stories to share who we are. We tell stories to discover who we are" (M. Blei, personal communication, March 2, 2019).

My seventh-grade social studies teacher has impacted my life because as he was helping us become better citizens, I started to become an activist because of it and care about current events. —Seventh grader

---

Storytelling helps students develop as listeners. Jennifer Aaker (as cited in Rush, 2014), a marketing professor at Stanford's Graduate School of Business, says, "Our brains are wired to understand and retain stories. . . . A story is a journey that moves the listener, and when the listener goes on that journey they feel different." Teachers can obtain resources (https://themoth.org/education/teachers) about how to teach and encourage students to tell their stories, and sign up as a curriculum partner to obtain even more comprehensive resources and reproducible handouts. The Moth hosts live, often themed events around the United States in which people tell true personal stories live.

Many of these ideas and strategies extend far beyond storytelling, and teachers can use them in the classroom as icebreakers, relationship builders, and to forge connections and build community. The most effective strategies geared toward developing speakers and listeners are designed to help students craft a personal true story to share with the class through oral storytelling. The art and craft of oral storytelling require a departure from the traditional story arc. In a way, an oral story is similar to a podcast in that it has a predictable structure to help the listeners follow the story. The Moth offers a story map to teachers who sign up as curriculum partners at their website; students use the story map as a guide as they craft their oral stories. Planning for oral storytelling is a good example of designing with the end in mind, because the classroom culture teachers work so deliberately to build will ultimately support students for this kind of share.

Micaela sees storytelling in the classroom not only as a way to help students develop as speakers and listeners but also as a way to bring students' lives into the classroom to foster engagement. She talks about how when students' stories are a part of the classroom experience, it creates a sense of belonging because students know, "If I'm not here, the whole class isn't here. My voice is essential to this room. My voice is essential to this class."

Storytelling builds on academic skills like "crafting a narrative, choosing details, identifying themes, and speaking so people will listen, and she also claims storytelling is "the most practical thing you can do in your classroom" because of the real-world application:

> If students can learn to shape a story with an awareness of who they are, what they are trying to get across and what they want their audience to understand, you are preparing students for job interviews, to write to shareholders, inspire a team, share research with potential funders . . . Storytelling in a classroom becomes a lab for authentic practice for being an excellent communicator. (M. Blei, personal communication, March 2, 2019)

Micaela was effusive in her examples of how storytelling is everywhere in the real world, including the master of science program in narrative medicine at Columbia

University, and how the ability of doctors to listen well can enable them to save patients' lives. The Columbia University School of Professional Studies (n.d.) website indicates:

> The care of the sick unfolds in stories. The effective practice of healthcare requires the ability to recognize, absorb, interpret, and act on the stories and plights of others. Medicine practiced with narrative competence is a model for humane and effective medical practice.

Micaela also clarifies how storytelling supports a student-centered classroom:

> When students work on a story to try and get closer to what is being heard and understood by a listener, they rely on the listener's reactions to decide what details to keep in and omit. In turn, the listener doesn't need to be an expert in narrative to guide the storyteller. (M. Blei, personal communication, March 2, 2019)

I learned another important guiding principle from the 2018 Moth Teacher Institute. One is to teach students that although a personal story can be very powerful, they should tell a story that "is a scar, not a wound." We discuss how a scar is something that is healed, and a wound is raw—it can be easily opened, reinjured, and cause pain. I explain to my students that when we tell stories we are not ready to tell, we not only risk further damaging ourselves but also making our audience uncomfortable as they suffer through our story with us and worry about our well-being. Yet, a story that is a "scar" can feel cathartic for the speaker and transformative for the listener.

I also remind students that when telling a story, the speaker should stay in his or her growth zone (stretching his or her ability) but stay out of the danger zone (which feels uncomfortable for both the speaker and the listener). As speakers we must be aware of our audience, much like when we write. Speakers have a benefit that writers do not because they can read the audience's body language and facial expressions to see how they are responding to the story. A speaker who is in tune with the audience can make adjustments based on this immediate feedback. As listeners whose brains are primed to respond to stories, we begin to share the emotions of the storyteller (Zak, 2014), so it is essential to not only carefully curate a story, but attend to the audience's reactions.

Beyond developing students' speaking and listening skills, storytelling encourages taking perspective, builds empathy, forges identity, and builds relationships and community in the classroom. To yield these benefits, students need guidance finding the story they most want or need to tell. Telling the right story can help students find meaning in a life struggle, and it can be cathartic to identify and share this realization with others. Teachers should remind students the story they choose doesn't define them, but it might just be the story they need to tell right now.

Show students a variety of the stories The Moth curates for the classroom, and if you, as the teacher, are willing, model your own story and share your process. Visit **go.SolutionTree.com/literacy** for links to storytelling resources. After students listen to many different stories, they will get a sense of what good oral storytelling sounds like. At this point, students can begin brainstorming possible story ideas by reflecting on prompts through writing, and The Moth (2016) curriculum guide has a comprehensive set of prompts to help students start thinking about the story they'd like to tell.

Ways to begin:

- People think I'm . . .
- One thing I never thought I'd do is . . .

At a time when:

- "Your beliefs were challenged or changed" (The Moth, 2016, p. 47)
- "You made a shocking discovery" (The Moth, 2016, p. 47)

Once students have a few story ideas, they can test them on their peers in small groups; often conversations with others inspire their best ideas. When students are ready with a story idea, I offer The Moth's (2016) framework from their curriculum guide for organizing and telling a story.

Before students perform their oral stories (or any kind of presentation or share), I ask my students to use a supportive warm-up activity from the comedy improvisation world, specifically the Magnet Theater in New York City (M. Blei, personal communication, March 2, 2019). Storytellers stand in a group, and individually say to one another, "Got your back." The recipient of this reassuring phrase repeats it back. This statement is coupled with a gentle pat on the shoulder or another supportive gesture that doesn't involve physical contact. I tell my students in advance this may feel awkward at first, but they intuitively understand the supportive nature of the act. It also serves as our common language—a reassuring phrase we use throughout the school year.

Regardless of the speaking and listening opportunity, teachers need to design backward from the learning outcomes to ensure students achieve the desired goals. For example, students can perform stories in front of a whole class or share them in small groups. One positive aspect of students telling stories in randomly selected small groups is intimacy and connection. In this instance, we can guide students to the understanding we are all storytellers and compassionate listeners when we hear something worth listening to. If the teacher wants to ensure he or she listens to all students' stories, a whole-class event is the way to go. When students perform stories in front of the whole class, you can put them more at ease by grading them on a written format of their story based on criteria established beforehand; for example, you might assess that they followed the story map and that their story achieves the desired impact. This type of assessment allows you to attend oral storytelling events as a listener rather than an assessor, which students appreciate.

The act of storytelling meets many common state standards because it requires students to speak for different purposes and audiences, and consider how to use narrative structure and technique to craft their delivery.

Assessments

To further support student conversations, I sometimes insert myself into these discussions, not as the teacher, but as a conversationalist who asks a provocative question to turn or deepen the conversation, or as an advisor to provide a gentle correction. I leave my gradebook behind, and resist the temptation to dominate the conversation or engage in a minilecture. Instead, I sit in a student desk or roll up a chair to join them as a curious participant. Then, students will welcome the intervention to enhance the conversation. Another strategy to elevate a conversation is to distribute a quotation or short reading at a pivotal point in the conversation to introduce a controversial idea or new perspective to challenge students' initial findings.

Teachers need to be mindful; grading can stifle the quality of an authentic conversation, and consequently, hinder students' progress. Re-evaluate traditional grading practices like grading students on how many times they speak, and if they use textual evidence to support their points, build on other students' comments, and draw other students into the conversation. These attributes are worthy of consideration, but they tend to breed compliance rather than foster curiosity, interest, or the desire to clarify one's own (or someone else's) thinking, which is essential to the authentic practice of speaking and listening skills.

Furthermore, the desire for a particular grade and eagerness to share their most compelling arguments can lead students to engage in what amounts to minipresentations. We've all likely heard a student say, "To add on . . . , " but instead of elaborating on another student's point, the student shares a completely new idea. This type of behavior indicates the student wasn't listening, but simply waiting for a pause in the conversation to meet certain criteria and secure the desired grade. Grading these discussions can, at the same time, create a false proxy for speaking and become a hindrance for listening.

One way to formatively assess a discussion as well as build students' capacity for reflection is to have groups stop to consider their progress during the discussion. If groups are sharing simultaneously, the teacher can signal the whole class to pause, and pose questions that cause students to *process* the process and discuss the quality of their discussion thus far. These can be simple questions like the following.

- "How are we doing?"
- "What did we do well?"
- "What didn't we do well?"
- "What can we improve?"
- "Has everyone had the opportunity to contribute equally?"
- "What goals can we set going forward?"

This mid-discussion reflection not only offers the teacher valuable information (especially if multiple discussions are occurring simultaneously) but also allows groups to set new goals before resuming the discussion. If teachers want a more formal assessment of a student-led discussion, one method is to require students to complete a written reflection upon completion (figure 6.6).

Prior to the Discussion
My current speaking goal for this school year is:
I intend to work toward this goal during this discussion by:
My current listening goal for this school year is:
I intend to work toward this goal during this discussion by:
What viewpoints do you anticipate others to introduce during the discussion that are in opposition to your own?
After the Discussion
How well did you do in reaching your speaking and listening goals?
Summary: What were some of the key ideas covered during the discussion?
Reaction: Write down a comment you remember from the discussion. What about this comment resonated with you? Do you agree or disagree with it? Does it raise more questions?
Reflection: What is it about your own position that gives you trouble? What is it about an opposing position of another that attracts you? How did the discussion influence your thinking about the topic or text? What progress did you make toward your speaking and listening goals?

Thinking Ahead: Did you gain one new opinion or insight as a result of the discussion? What lingering questions do you have worthy of further exploration?
Goal Setting: Identify a personal goal to improve on your performance for the next discussion.

Figure 6.6: Student-led discussion reflection questions.

Visit **go.SolutionTree.com/literacy** for a free reproducible version of this figure.

While Students Are Working

When students are working, the teacher's role is to encourage, redirect, ask questions, and celebrate. Teachers can introduce new information and concepts if they will enhance the work students are doing or help them make connections with other learning and their lives. Once the teacher sets the foundation for an activity, it is his or her job to decide what each student needs to reach his or her highest potential; the teacher does this by being curious and listening. Provide opportunities for self-assessment throughout the process, reflection on completion, and goal setting for the future.

My sixth-grade science teacher asked me to present my project in front of other classes. He didn't make a big deal about it, which made me think that he really chose my project because it was good. This also helped me stop thinking that I was a bad presenter. He never made it seem like it was one of my weaknesses at all. —Seventh grader

Second Chances and Do-Overs

Reading and writing may come with their own challenges, but speaking opportunities tend to trigger students' nerves like no other. Many students would prefer to spend the majority of their school career ensconced safely behind a desk far away from the front of the room or far away from discussions without the security of the teacher. As much as teachers may feel their classroom environment provides a safe place for students to take risks, they must be open to the possibility that some students may not be ready to complete every activity in the same way as their peers. I may not explicitly offer alternatives for speaking activities because I don't want to provide easy ways out, but my students know me well enough to know I'm here to help if they're struggling.

When I give an assignment that I know involves more risk and requires vulnerability, I say something like, "If you take this home and realize you need to run something by me, send me an email and we'll figure it out. I know if I had to do this assignment, I might be unsure about how to begin." I also offer times I'm available for private conversations. I also find it helpful to invite students inside my thinking with something like, "When I first thought about how I would do this assignment, my first idea was ________, which I still think is a good idea, but it made me uncomfortable. So then I changed it to ________, which felt a lot better." As often as possible, I complete the student assignments, not only so I can model the assignment, but so I can share insight into my process—where I struggled, what I learned, and how I challenged myself to grow. The only way I can learn about this process is to do the assignment myself.

Students have sought out the opportunity to complete recitations and other speaking opportunities privately, with only me as an audience, or by creating a video or presentation. To ensure these reluctant students make steady progress over the year, I slowly increase their audience. The student and I devise a plan and reach some mutual agreements as to what he or she feels comfortable to try. The student then continually revisits and reflects on his or her speaking and listening goals. Here, again, I ask students, "How can you get out of your comfort zone, yet stay in your growth zone?" and "What is your plus-one?"

My third-grade teacher always told me to stand up for myself because although I was a very loud person, I wasn't really good at standing up for myself. I would stand up for others, but I was too scared to do it for myself. She taught me that it is important to speak out. I think it helped me, over the years, become a more confident speaker. —Seventh grader

Teachers can challenge and continually signal students to reflect on their speaking and listening goals throughout the year. If teachers don't give students second chances, they are missing a valuable opportunity to help students grow and develop the skills they so desperately need. Wormeli (2011) contends the repeated practice of essential skills is how adults achieve mastery:

> Adult professionals actually flourish through redos, retakes, and do-overs. Surgeons practice on cadavers before doing surgeries on live patients. Architects redesign building plans until they meet all the specifications listed. Pilots rehearse landings and takeoffs hundreds of times in simulators and in solo flights before flying with real passengers. Lawyers

practice debate and analysis of arguments before litigating real cases.

Second chances and do-overs don't necessarily have to mean extra work for the teacher but can be exactly what students need to achieve mastery. I offer a second chance, when they are ready, for students who become unexpectedly nervous in the middle of a speaking activity. Often, they are able to compose themselves after a few more students take their turn, or the student resumes their turn the next class. For students to not mistake my kindness for weakness, students must request a smaller audience or different medium well in advance. Students who arrive with excuses on the day of a presentation are considered unprepared.

When I offer second chances, I worry very little about which students are actually making excuses or not working to their ability. It is abundantly clear to my students that I am devoted to helping them grow as learners, but that if they don't apply themselves with honesty and integrity, then I cannot help them. I choose to believe that every student cares about being a better communicator and a more literate citizen.

For students to develop as speakers and listeners, teachers must fully grasp their role in the classroom—architects of an intricate design constructed well before students enter. Once the "beams and scaffolds" are laid and secure, teachers can intentionally strengthen the foundation of the classroom design through words, actions, choices, activities, and even assessments. If teachers create experiences for students to encourage the practice of the critical thinking skills most standards demand for speaking and listening, they prepare students to be better skilled in building meaningful relationships and becoming the kind of articulate and engaged citizens the world needs.

Questions for Reflection

Consider these questions after reading the chapter.

How have the ideas in this chapter caused me to re-evaluate some of my teaching practices, and what strategies would I change, and how?

____

____

How can I incorporate the benefits of storytelling in my classroom in a way that aligns with my course content and learning outcomes?

____

____

What activities in this chapter align with my course content and learning outcomes and would develop students as speakers and listeners?

____

____

What other questions do I have?

____

____

So I just listened, my pen in the air.
—Mary Oliver

Listening With an Ear Toward the Future

Being a teacher comes with the daunting responsibility of educating other people's children and the power to affect them for the rest of their lives. I try not to think about this too much, or I probably wouldn't be able to get myself to school in the morning. The pressure to do this job well can feel crushing, but the results of doing this job well are immeasurable. After over twenty years' experience as a teacher, there are so many things I am still uncertain about. The only way I've been able to manage this perpetual state of uneasiness is to learn to feel comfortable with the questions, and to know that the answers are ever-changing and exist just beyond me. Suddenly, hesitation becomes wonder, and this shift in mindset opens me to listen to my students, my colleagues, and the research without feeling threatened or unmoored but instead challenged and inspired.

I do hold tightly to the few things I'm sure of: as a teacher, my role is to design learning experiences that place students at the center and provide them with opportunities to practice the skills and dispositions they need to engage thoughtfully with the world. My job is to create a space in which students feel safe and valued, and to do the important work together that is meaningful to their lives. I believe all of this begins with a relationship and a sense of belonging.

When I was in fourth grade, I had a teacher who was fun. She was so good at making students feel heard, even though many of us didn't have much to say at age nine. If something didn't go as well as you thought it would, she'd give you every opportunity to understand and learn from your mistakes. If you had an idea, she'd listen to it. She made me feel like I wasn't just another student. —Ninth grader

Our students' emotional lives are intimately connected to their ability to engage in the work we are doing together. Skill and drill, coupled with quiet compliance, is not the way to graduate the kind of future citizens our world needs. At the same time, the most well-designed problem-based learning task won't effectively cause learning if the conditions for engagement don't exist. According to neuroscientist Richard Davidson (as cited in Tippett, 2019c), "Thought and feeling are absolutely intermingled in the brain, and so there are no areas of the brain that are exclusively dedicated to one and not the other."

For learning to occur, teachers must ensure students feel safe, accepted, and valued. We need to personally connect with them, and they need to feel emotionally invested in the work we are doing in our classrooms. If we can't connect to their emotional lives, students are pulled instead by insecurities, the fear of grades, and social pressures. Relationships and belonging are a prerequisite to engagement, which is essential for learning, and they are the fundamental ingredients that bring joy to teaching and learning, which benefit all of us. By embracing our vulnerability, trying new strategies, and considering the mindset offered in this book, we can open ourselves to be changed by the emotional lives of our students on their journey to becoming better readers, writers, speakers, and listeners. In so many ways, it is our students who hold the answers to the question, What will make us more effective teachers?

At the end of the year, I ask students to reflect on the work they did during the year so they can consolidate what they've learned, determine what they did well and what they can do differently next time, and how they would like to move forward. We have a share day called Our Greatest Hits. I want students to know how much I value their reflection, so we dedicate thirty minutes of class time for writing and exploring the following prompts as a way to guide them for their final writer's notebook entry (figure E.1).

Directions: Think about the work you've done this year and consider the following questions.

- What were some important lessons you learned?
- What work did you do that you are most proud of?
- Of the work we did together this year, what would you most like to share with others?

Review our Quotes of the Week, Google Classroom assignments, your writing on Google Drive (https://google.com/drive), your writer's notebook entries, and our speaking and listening opportunities, as well as moments from class this year—discussions, comments from your peers, moments of insight, and others.

After reflecting, what are three pieces you might like to share?

Figure E.1: Our Greatest Hits from the school year reflective prompts.

Visit **go.SolutionTree.com/literacy** for a free reproducible version of this figure.

My fifth-grade teacher positively impacted my life. He would put daily sticky notes on our desk which contained messages of hope and encouragement. He would also offer morning tutoring in school, which really helped me and all of my other peers. —Ninth grader

I look forward to live music, Echoes Projects, raps inspired by Hughes's (2001) "Theme for English B," dramatic performances, and paired analyses and connections between book excerpts and plays that anchor our year. One student expressed a desire to create something new out of her favorite Quotes of the Week, and another student wants to assemble pivotal quotes across various works of literature to express a universal theme. I look forward to ending each school year with the affirmation that my students learned what they most needed to know, and I gave them the inspiration and the space to do so. These shares inform my teaching because they give me an authentic sense of what worked for my students and the opportunity to revisit some of the lessons that perhaps didn't seem to resonate as much. Our Greatest Hits, of course, incentivize listening because when students share their most meaningful lessons from the school year, they are beyond worth listening to.

APPENDIX
Teachers' Stories

I am endlessly curious to hear more about how relationships with students, classroom culture, and personalized learning experiences impact student behavior, achievement, and literacy. Hearing the stories in this appendix affirmed my belief that focusing on relationships and belonging and listening to our students and each other are the ways to improve not only literacy skills, but student learning and their lives.

Each of the following stories begins with a relationship and a teacher who worked earnestly to determine how to best meet the needs of an individual student with the ultimate goal of impacting learning.

Jennifer Bard, Special Education, West Windsor-Plainsboro High School North

Jennifer Bard is a special education teacher with a specialty in language arts at West Windsor-Plainsboro High School North in Plainsboro, New Jersey. She runs a job program for special education students with learning differences. Her students intern at a fitness center, the school district's food services department, a packaging center, a nature preserve, and in the district (as a teacher's assistant in the younger grades). Jennifer is steadfast and kind, and at the same time, she holds her students to a high standard; they love and appreciate her for it. Her hope is for these internships to help her students forge connections in the world, so they will have people and possibly even jobs they can rely on when they graduate from high school (J. Bard, personal communication, November 1, 2018).

> *I had a student, Josh, who struggled with his already far-below-grade-level reading and writing skills. Josh struggled not only with engagement during class but also with attendance. School was understandably frustrating and not his favorite place to be. He was generally unmotivated; freshman year, he completely shut down and wouldn't even do the work. However, Josh did stay in class and listen, and eventually became engaged and asked for help. He came to me often for extra help during study hall.*
>
> *There was a time when Josh didn't feel like going to his internship. The bus was ready to leave, but he told me he just didn't feel like going, and then asked me if I ever wanted to take a day off. I explained, "We all make choices,*

and your choices result in consequences. You're eighteen years old. You need to make this decision." I agonized as I left Josh to make the decision, but my heart soared when he got on the bus.

A mechanical pencil has become a metaphor for our connection. During Josh's freshman year, I wrote with a particular kind of mechanical pencil and he loved it. I told him if he was going to do work, he could have the pencil. Josh never lost the pencil, and together we refilled it with lead. When he turned eighteen, I wanted to do something special for him, so I presented him with a mechanical pencil and note (figure A.1). The smile on Josh's face showed me how much it meant to him.

Figure A.1: Showing students they matter.

I work with students who find school work hard, and their behavior in school reflects their frustration and lack of motivation. I see through this, and even when it's not easy (and often, it's not), I knows these are precisely the students who need me most. They need to connect with one person. Just one person can make a difference in a student's life. Now, I am the teacher students come to visit, stay in contact with, and invite to their weddings. I change their lives.

My sixth-grade social studies teacher taught me that it was OK to be me. She helped me through hard times and always knew when something was wrong. She was someone I could talk to about anything because she never judged. She made school easier and made everything doable. —Seventh grader

---

Marla Fruhling, Third Grade, Maurice Hawk Elementary School

Marla's story about the dedication required to determine how to engage a struggling reader and writer transcends grade levels. Her story clearly exemplifies how paying attention and listening to our students build relationships and trust and how, on this strong foundation, students can take the risks required to build literacy skills (M. Fruhling, personal communication, October 13, 2018).

> *Relationships and classroom community are everything in my third-grade classroom. It's easy to get swept up in curriculum and pacing guide demands, or the fact that we, as teachers, never have as much time as we'd like to teach. I've found, however, that without intentionally spending time on knowing my students as individuals, only a fraction of my students' potential can be reached. One school year, my student, Miles, proved how much impact relationships and classroom climate can have on learning.*
>
> *While Miles was fun-loving, friendly, and gentle, he wasn't very loud or outgoing. If I'm being honest, he was the kind of student I could imagine easily falling through the cracks. When Miles started third grade with me, I did the same thing that I always do at the beginning of the year. I focused on learning about each of my students, helping him or her learn about one another, and setting up routines. I noticed quickly that some of my students—especially Miles—weren't particularly interested in reading or writing.*
>
> *Within the first few weeks of school that year, I strategically chose lower-risk activities which invited all students to participate. As we became more comfortable with one another, I increased the risk. Once I got to know my students and they got to know one another through daily morning meetings, brain breaks, short games, and icebreakers, it was time to get to know each student as an individual. When I offered students choices, I paid attention to the kind of choices each student made to learn what motivated him or her. I communicated with my students' families early and frequently to learn their values and hopes for their child. So much of teaching is just paying attention. Sometimes we need to stop acting and only listen. This is how I began to get to know Miles.*
>
> *Just as I had noticed at the beginning of the year, Miles was still not excited about reading or writing. Some teachers might have described him as a reluctant writer and reader. He entered third grade reading below benchmark, and he avoided writing as much as possible. I felt that I had built a solid relationship with Miles as a person, but now I had to build my relationship with him through a literacy lens. He needed to know that he was a member of our writing and reading communities specifically, not just our class community.*

It started with almost-daily reading and writing conferences. Each day in a reader's and writer's workshop, Miles and I worked to build his skill set. When I met with him and asked him what he was working on as a reader or writer, I'd listen and take notes. When I tried to swoop in with a teaching point, he'd listen, try the strategy, and then abandon it soon after our conference ended. This continued for a few weeks, and I was stumped. Why wouldn't Miles use the strategies I was teaching him independently after our conferences? He was perfectly capable; he showed me during our conferences that he could use the skills. It didn't seem like Miles independently viewed himself as a reader or writer.

I maintained the same strategy until the end of December. Meanwhile, I was reaching out to learning consultants and scouring the internet for ideas. I had "lunch munch" with Miles and some of his classmates a few times (something I do with all students to build our community). I played with him and his classmates at recess, and I sent home a handful of positive emails and notes recognizing his efforts. I provided lots of choice—he could read any book he wanted, write about any topic within a genre he wanted, and could pick any seat in our flexible seating learning environment. I purchased books he was interested in, and showed him where they were in our library. I think I proved to Miles that I cared about him and would never give up on him, but I wasn't reaching him as a reader or writer yet. He was progressing, but not enough. He was still below benchmark. I knew I needed to try something different.

I decided to stop "teaching" Miles for a while, and instead, just compliment him. I had built a community in my classroom as a whole, but maybe I needed to work on bringing Miles into our literacy community. When I'd confer with Miles, I'd ask him what he was working on as a reader or writer (as I always did). When he answered, I'd find something he had already done that was great, and I'd tell him why it was important for readers and writers to do that. I'd stop there, and simply move onto another conference with another student.

Then, I started highlighting Miles as the "expert" based on what he reported to me when I was holding table conferences with small groups. In a traditional table conference, the teacher finds a student demonstrating a skill well, shares about it with other students working in the same area, and asks others to practice the same skill. I also highlighted Miles's work in the closure portion of lessons, and I included copied portions of his writer's notebook on our class charts if they illustrated an example we were learning about together.

After a few weeks, I could see Miles's demeanor change during reading and writing. When he sensed a conference coming, he'd sit up straighter, read with more facial expressions, or write a little faster. When I ended a conference with a classmate, he'd look at me hopefully. This was new! Miles liked talking with me before, but I didn't exactly see him as eager to have a conference. This change in him told me that Miles's confidence was the missing piece. It didn't matter that Miles was always capable of the work because he didn't feel he was capable of the work.

Now that Miles was viewing himself as a member of our reading and writing communities, he was taking more academic risks in class and building momentum. Because he felt more confident, I was able to talk about what challenged Miles without disrupting his progress. We decided together (perhaps with some gentle suggesting on my part) that using a timer might be a helpful tool for improving as a writer. He could focus on one task at a time while the timer was on. By breaking his writing into smaller, more achievable tasks, writing became less overwhelming to him. I had already modeled how writers make plans for their writing and then follow through with their plans, but using a timer to focus on just one aspect eased Miles's discomfort. It was important to introduce it in this way and not as a deadline or time limit.

That year, I continually highlighted Miles as an expert, and I never stopped listening. He finished the year above benchmark in both reading and writing. He read books and wrote comics for fun. Figuring out what Miles needed in order to learn, instead of following the traditional path that worked with most of my students, made all of the difference in his success as a reader and writer.

One teacher who made a difference in my life was my first-grade teacher. She was a very nice woman that taught me to accept other people even if we had differing views. (She was a Red Sox fan, and I was a Yankees fan.) This has helped me throughout the rest of my life to be accepting and kind. —Seventh grader

---

Ellin Glassband, Language Arts, West Windsor-Plainsboro High School South

Ellin Glassband is a language arts teacher at West Windsor-Plainsboro High School South in West Windsor, New Jersey. She has co-taught for almost twenty years with Stacey Tafoya, who is a special education teacher, and works as an in-class resource (E. Glassband, personal communication, October 10, 2018).

Deeksha was rarely able to come to school and if she did, she usually did not make it through the day. She was painfully shy and quiet in class, and often looked like she wanted to disappear. My co-teacher Stacey and I dedicated ourselves to making some kind of a connection with Deeksha and creating a classroom environment where she felt safe and secure.

We would check in, have private conversations, praise her work (which was often of the highest caliber), and slowly began to pair her with patient, wonderful students for collaborative assignments. By the middle of the year, Deeksha was coming to class every day and soon after that, she even began to participate. We devoted ourselves to forming a positive relationship with her in- and outside class. It became clear that Deeksha was starting to feel more comfortable and, dare I say it, even happy to be in class! She began to take academic risks, which showed a growing self-assurance in her writing that was lacking earlier in the year. Her parents and outside therapists often let us know how much she enjoyed coming to class, and it showed.

One of the very last assignments of the year for that class was a memorized monologue from Hamlet, *complete with costumes, gestures, and movements. It's a challenging task for any ninth-grade student, but Deeksha was a particular concern of ours. Again, Stacey and I did all we could to boost her confidence. We met with her outside class, and even gave her the option of performing privately just for us. To our amazement, Deeksha said she was ready. Despite the tremendous improvement in her writing and attendance, an assignment like this was extremely daunting and anxiety provoking for Deeksha. I must admit that all these years later, I still get a bit choked up when I think of her, volunteering to perform on day one, in full garb, and not only presenting a masterful and flawless dramatic performance, but memorizing twice as many lines as was required. This performance came from a student who barely uttered a word for the first nine weeks of class. Deeksha's classmates exploded in applause, a communal recognition of how far she had come.*

The story could end there, but to my delight, two years later, Deeksha enrolled in my junior-level honors course. She and I had maintained our relationship over the years, and I knew she had continued to work on herself and seek outside help, which helped her blossom into an even more confident young woman. She was one of the top students in my junior class that year. I've been teaching for twenty-six years, and although I've had many poignant moments with students over the years, Deeksha serves as a reminder of the vital importance of letting our students know how much they matter, how valued they are, and how committed we are to their success.

My art teacher has been one of my closest teachers since I first came to middle school, not only because of our common love for art but because sharing our life matters with each other. She also eagerly listens to whatever I have to say, may it be happy or sad. Sometimes, I also complain about big tests that I'm worried about and she will encourage me to do well. —Seventh grader

---

Kaitlin Maher, Seventh-Grade Language Arts, Community Middle School

Kaitlin Maher is a language arts teacher at Community Middle School in West Windsor, New Jersey. She shares a story about a boy she calls Frankie, who taught her during her third year as a teacher how knowing her students can make all of the difference in their ability to achieve (K. Maher, personal communication, November 20, 2018).

I remember my first day of school with Frankie. Our middle school team decided to kick off the year with a variety of collaborative and fun activities so our students could not only get to know one another, but in my mind, give us a first impression of who they are. During times when my fellow colleagues and I were trying to infuse some excitement into our students about a sense of team, Frankie pulled away from the group and stayed toward the back close to the one other boy he knew. He would not stop talking and refused to listen. When I asked him to quiet down, he rolled his eyes and talked back. I thought to myself, "Well, this will be a fun year."

Soon after, the other teachers and I had our first team meeting with our school's guidance counselor. I learned that Frankie's father was a firefighter and, due to job-related complications, he had a stroke that caused brain damage. Frankie's father lived in a nursing home. Frankie was only able to see him when his mother, a hard-working nurse, was able to take him there. I lost my own mother at eighteen, so my heart immediately connected to this child's. I thought of all I had experienced, and that this child knew this pain at eleven years old. I was immediately ashamed of myself as an educator and a human being. How could I not realize that everyone has a story? I should have realized that this student had one too and wondered about why this boy acted the way he did instead of judging him for doing so.

Aside from learning about Frankie's family situation, the guidance counselor also informed me that he hated reading and writing. I immediately made a decision that it would not be the case this year. Over the next few weeks, I began to get to know Frankie. I asked him questions. When he wore a sports jersey, I talked teams with him. I would ask that class of students what the cool new music was so they could help me "stay young," which was one of the questions he was willing to answer. I learned he loved dogs, and I researched different titles I thought would interest him. We found books about service dogs that helped the military. He bought himself a book like this one at the book fair, and I purchased books for my classroom that I thought he would enjoy reading.

When it came time to write his realistic fiction story, I taught a lesson called Growing Wishes Into Realistic Fiction Ideas. For this lesson, the students come up with three realistic wishes that could possibly come true by the end of the school year and then choose one of those wishes to write their story about. I have learned so much about my students from this lesson over the past few years. I learned that one student never owned a bike; his family simply could not afford it. (When I told my colleagues, we all chipped in and bought him his very first bike for Christmas that year.) I also learned that early in the year, many students are afraid to share anything more than a superficial wish, so I do get many responses like, "Go viral on YouTube" or "Get a new phone." But I also learned from the student who suffered with eczema that she longed "to feel comfortable in her own skin" and from another that he hoped "to improve my pronunciation and my stutter." From Frankie, I learned that his greatest wish was to have a dog, and Frankie ultimately decided to write a story about a boy who had never owned a dog. Frankie decided the boy in the story would have to prove to his mother that he could get better grades and become more responsible. Only then might she think about getting a dog. I told Frankie I loved this idea. I nudged him and said, "Hey, you never know, maybe if you work really hard on this story, your mom will be so impressed, and you'll get that dog someday."

Frankie was the most engaged I've ever seen him. He wrote. He asked questions. He accepted feedback. He even actually started to become more responsible, as he cathartically wrote his story, in real life. He was the main character, and in writing about it, he became it.

When it came time to submit the realistic fiction stories in early December, I eagerly pulled Frankie's from my dense pile to read it. Though his grammar wasn't perfect, he had a heart-warming story with a fully developed character and of course, a happy ending. I was so proud that I reached out to his mother and told her about how hard he was working in class and about this touching story he wrote. I shared his story with her, and she thanked me for helping and sharing.

On our return to school in January, Frankie ran into class, approaching me! He was ecstatic to share that for Christmas, he got a puppy. The puppy was a German shepherd—just like the one he read about in one of our classroom books.

I tell Frankie's story every year when I teach my Growing Wishes Into Realistic Fiction Ideas lesson. His story is the quintessential model of a great story—one of hope, perseverance, and increased perspective, complete with a wish that actually came true. After what I learned from Frankie, I try to remind myself that when a student is disorganized, disinterested, even disrespectful—there is a story there. There is always a story. I still get frustrated, but I try to take a deep breath, step back for a minute, and first ask the student, "Are you having a bad day?" Sometimes he or she will say "What?" most likely thinking to him- or herself, "Wait a second—am I not in trouble?" And then, the answer I almost always get is yes.

Maybe our students are having a bad day, or maybe we just let them get away with something. Sometimes students give me a yes *followed by tears and, in that moment, I know it was the right question to ask. A simple question can build a connection with a student and let him or her know I'm here. I care. I will listen if you need to talk, and I will hand you a tissue if you need to cry. Kids need that. Don't we all?*

In my seventh-grade math class we had a choice for our projects, and when you choose something that you're interested in, the work always turns out to be better. —Ninth grader

---

Ashley Warren, World Language, West Windsor-Plainsboro High School North

Ashley Warren is a world language teacher at West Windsor-Plainsboro High School North in Plainsboro, New Jersey. Ashley shares a story about how a relationship and a personalized learning experience led to a Guinness world record (A. Warren, personal communication, October 16, 2018).

I remember the first time that I ever saw Sid in school. I was observing a colleague's fourth-grade Spanish class as she conducted a whole-class discussion. Each time she asked a question, Sid's hand flew into the air. Again and again, Sid's hand shot up, and a look of impatience and determination marked his young face when his name was not called. I noticed Sid seemed frustrated when my colleague called on other students, and I chuckled when I saw Sid mumbling to himself, correcting his peers' errors. At nine years old, I could tell Sid was an exceptionally gifted student. I could also tell Sid struggled to relate to his peers.

I continued to see Sid in the halls long after that class observation. Sid never initiated conversation, and it soon became clear to me that Sid found it hard to interact with adults as well. But sometimes, if I was lucky, Sid would speak to me. Why me? If I learned anything about Sid in that class observation, it was that he wanted to practice his Spanish. And I, an elementary Spanish teacher, was a willing conversation partner. So, from time to time, Sid and I would exchange brief conversaciones in the hallway.

Years later, I moved from my district's elementary school to the high school. Much to my surprise, one year, I walked into class on the first day of school and saw Sid sitting in the front row. As soon as we began our icebreaker, Sid's hand flew into the air. I had to stop myself from laughing. I could hardly believe how little Sid had changed. Sure, Sid was older, much taller, and sporting a deeper voice, but he was still that same gifted child who was over-eager to participate.

Sid's passion for Spanish had grown in the intervening years, and he had become an even more competent Spanish speaker, reader, and writer.

By the time he reached my class as a ninth grader, he was tackling topics twelfth graders struggled to master. By the spring, I'd grown accustomed to planning alternate activities for Sid and working one-on-one to more appropriately challenge him. Fortunately, the spring assessment for our technology unit allowed for a lot of student choice, and I knew Sid would shine.

The assessment was modeled after the TV show Shark Tank *(Burnett, Spirko, Fuchs, & Carter, 2009), so the students needed to create an invention and then use their Spanish skills to persuade a panel of "sharks" to vote for their invention. I told the students the invention with the most votes would secure a prize of the inventor's choice. Sid immediately began working on his project with fervor, and I could tell he wanted to win.*

I spent the next several class periods meeting with student inventors, listening to their design ideas, editing their early drafts, and supporting their linguistic needs. When I checked in with Sid, he told me he was building a laser that would burst balloons. I assumed, like many of the other students' designs, that his was a hypothetical invention. I was wrong. Unbeknownst to me, Sid went home and built a high-powered laser strong enough to burst balloons and ignite small fires. He then spray-painted a foam rubber gun black and mounted the laser on top of the toy gun.

On the day Sid was scheduled to enter the "Shark Tank," he arrived at school with his invention, which, it turns out, looked like a very real and very dangerous weapon. He wasn't in the building more than a few minutes when school administrators confiscated his project. I quickly found myself sitting with an inconsolable Sid and his guidance counselor. The counselor explained that Sid's weapon was being held in the principal's office. His face fell. There was talk of notifying the police. Someone called Sid's parents. Sid stared off blankly, seemingly unable to process what had happened.

Finally, Sid looked up at me with tears in his eyes and said, "Now there's no chance I'll win the Shark Tank." My heart broke. He wasn't thinking about the principal, the police, or his parents. He was devastated that he wouldn't be able to present his project and potentially win the Shark Tank competition.

As a teacher, I felt like I had betrayed him. I had encouraged him to build whatever he wanted. And because Sid was so driven and so talented, I had not checked in on him as much as I had the other kids. I didn't even know Sid knew how to build lasers! Had I known he was going to bring a fire-starting laser to school, I could have intervened. But, I didn't. So there we sat, half listening to the counselor who tried to explain why this was a danger, why Sid needed to be more careful, and so on.

After we left the counselor's office, I told Sid I was proud of his creativity. And I assured him we would find a way for him to still participate in the competition. Sid's face lit up. For the first time that day, I saw hope in his eyes. After consulting with Sid's parents, we decided he would film himself presenting the laser invention at home, and then show the video at school.

As it turns out, Sid was also very good at making videos, so his final presentation really impressed his peers. So much so, the class voted Sid the winner of Shark Tank. I'll never forget Sid's smile.

I got to see Sid smile a lot over the next three years. As a sophomore, he took the AP Spanish language exam and earned college credit. As a junior, he wrote a satirical poem in my Spanish literature class that was published in a collegiate literary magazine. As a senior, he enjoyed teaching minilessons as a teacher's assistant in my Spanish 1 class. From time to time, we'd reminisce and laugh about that Shark Tank project.

Just before Sid graduated, he invited me to serve as a witness for his attempt to break a Guinness world record. I was honored! When I asked him what record he wanted to break, a smile crept across his face, and he said "Well, it involves popping balloons with a laser." I fought back tears. Turns out, the work Sid started during our Shark Tank project three years earlier actually led to a Guinness world record!

My computer teacher in third grade really inspired me. She would give me compliments, and that sort of made me realize, "I'm good at this. I like this." If not for her, I don't know if today I would be trying to be an engineer. —Ninth grader

---

Valerie Kearns, Social Studies, West Windsor-Plainsboro High School South

Valerie Kearns is a social studies teacher at West Windsor-Plainsboro High School South in West Windsor, New Jersey. Val teaches a course called Social and Economic Problems in American Society. She encourages students to learn from one another as they openly express their views and listen to others with an open mind (V. Kearns, personal communication, February 25, 2019).

In our class discussions, I have students identify areas in which they agree and clarify areas of disagreement. This helps the class determine the most appropriate and practical solutions for some of the societal problems we address in the curriculum.

On the first day of school, after explaining my classroom expectations and emphasizing this importance of being open minded and supportive of other class members, a student named Alessia came up to talk to me. Alessia explained that while she found the content of the course interesting, she felt she would be unable to keep her composure during class discussions since she was very passionate about political issues but more important, there was another outspoken student in class whose political views she found intolerable. My eyes lit up and I smiled at her while she was explaining this, and then I told her she needed to be in the class for those exact reasons.

I explained I would help her become more at ease disagreeing with others in a productive manner, and reminded Alessia that effective communication is a life skill students need to practice while still in school. It took a bit of convincing, but she decided to stay. Discussions the first few months were interesting, and I often played the intermediary to help Alessia rephrase her comments to make them more accessible to others for continued dialogue. I often met with her after class to allow her to vent when she was feeling frustrated, and to remind her again that she was building an important life skill despite her discomfort.

The first day Alessia raised her hand to admit to the class that she actually agreed with the student who had caused her so much angst felt like a major success. Over time, I began to observe Alessia actively listening to this student when he spoke and addressing him directly to try to understand his perspective and how it compared to her own. She thanked me at the end of the year for encouraging her to stay in the class and admitted that she had become good friends with the other student, even spending time with him outside class. In her course reflection, when asked one of the most important things she learned during the year, Alessia wrote, "To listen more to others and try to be more understanding of those with different views than me."

As teachers, I think we have the ability (and the responsibility) to build student confidence and model behaviors that will help students become successful not only while in the classroom but also for the rest of their lives. Students can learn valuable life lessons in our classrooms if we create the environment where they feel safe and supported to take risks and challenges.

In eighth grade, my English teacher truly connected with each student on a personal level, trying to understand us as individuals. This helped each student, including me, to feel heard, and as though I made a difference. It motivated me to do well in that class. —Ninth grader

Jonathan Ellingson, English and History, Falls City High School

Jonathan Ellingson is a teacher, listener, and storyteller from Falls City High School, in Falls City, Oregon. Jonathan shares a story about listening that taught me the significance of not only listening but also about being a person students will listen to. Here is a portion of our emails in which he tells me about his teaching philosophy, his students, and the story that reminded him of why he teaches (J. Ellingson, personal communication, September 22, 2018).

I've always valued stories in my classroom. When I don't know what to do, I tell a story. I share a lot of excerpts or paraphrases of things I am reading and excited about. And when someone asks, "Can I tell you a story?" I say yes, and I listen. Honestly, teaching conversational English in Hungary informs my teaching techniques and classroom feel; the goal is to get students talking 80 percent of the time.

In Hungary, the students stand up when the teacher enters the room, and then the teacher tells them when they can sit. Every day, I would play a game called Tell Me Something I Don't Know and when each student did, he or she could sit down. It became harder and harder as the year went on because you would learn so much about them: "Balazs, I know you have a cat and a brother, and you don't like dancing, and you want to be an F1 racer and you think . . . . " I enjoy listening and laughing, and when I hear a good detail, I write it down in front of them. I ask a lot of follow-up questions, and I've found that a lot of kids are surprised that I care so much.

I am pretty honest about my own insecurities and fears. I make mistakes and apologize a bunch. I am not heroic in many of the things I share with students, which seems to open doors. I share the things I love and am fascinated with, and when students know you love mushrooms, typewriters, fountain pens, lichen, acorns, pinecones, and discarded library books, they come to you with things to share. As a gift, I once received a pair of salamanders, which were placed on my desk with a note reading, "We thought you would really love these."

I laugh a lot. I recommend things. I ask kids what they think I should do in certain situations. I make a lot of mistakes—sometimes on purpose—so I can apologize and share how I was wrong. I rejoice in honest failures and things that don't work but seem like they should. We tell a lot of stories in my class. I encourage kids to write: "That would be a great song" or "Put that in a poem" or "Have you written that yet?" or "You should write that in a letter to someone," and I pester, pester, pester, pester them for more details. I had a student working on an essay about taking apart cars with a torque wrench. When I see a kid excited about a topic, I listen, ask questions, and take notes. I keep telling him or her I want to hear more.

One of my students asked me, "How are you a teacher when all you do is ask questions?"

Another student asked, "I had a weird thought the other day. You know how you're always writing down things we say?"

"Yes."

"What if we started writing down things you say?"

"Interesting idea. Some would even argue that's the reason you're in here!"

> *I try to create an atmosphere that is open and questioning and values listening to all angles of a story or issue. I try my best not to overtly editorialize and reserve judgment. I emphasize listening, freedom of speech, the First Amendment, the power of metaphors, and William Strunk Jr. and E. B. White's (1959) imperative, "Vigorous writing is concise" (p. ix). In my class it's, "Say anything, but say it well." I praise what I think is good. We write a lot of lists. One list we write is of communication heroes, who are people you respect or people you listen to. I can write hundreds of names of writers, artists, poets, pastors, friends, family, professors, and teachers. Mentally, when I assign this list, I often feel like I am trying to turn my class over to someone else, or like I'm saying, "Go, listen to those people." I always envision noble and excellent people on the list—Jesus, Socrates, Martin Luther King Jr., E. B. White, Ira Glass. But sometimes I look at students' lists and my stomach turns because I am afraid these are the only voices they are truly listening to. And sometimes I see my name on these lists of people I don't respect at all, people I struggle to find common ground with. Sometimes looking at these lists stops me in my tracks.*
>
> *I often ask myself why I teach. Why bother? Couldn't someone else do it better? And it's in these moments I realize I teach because I'm sometimes on those lists and the work is not done. In some respects, I've helped give some kids communication skills they are preparing to use in nefarious ways. If I have the honor of being listened to (and being included on some students' lists), when most other voices won't get through, I better be someone worth listening to. I also better have values worth emulating. Values like listening.*

These teachers give me hope; my students give me hope. Hope is not optimism or wishful thinking. Hope is action and change. Hope is muscle and movement. Hope is teaching and learning. As teachers, I think we have much to be hopeful about, and one way we can continue to remain hopeful is to listen.

Questions for Reflection

Consider these questions after reading the appendix.

What ideas from this chapter can help me change my teaching practice to further relationship building, belonging, and student-centeredness?

____

____

In what ways do the educational research or teacher stories offer ideas or feel reassuring?

____

____

What stories from this book resonate with me or help renew or inspire me as a teacher?

____

____

References and Resources

Adichie, C. N. (2009, July). *Chimamanda Ngozi Adichie: The danger of a single story* [Video file]. Accessed at https://ted.com/talks/chimamanda_adichie_the_danger_of_a_single_story on February 9, 2019.

Ahmed, S. K. (2018). *Being the change: Lessons and strategies to teach social comprehension*. Portsmouth, NH: Heinemann.

Alexie, S. (2007). *The absolutely true diary of a part-time Indian*. New York: Little, Brown.

Allen, M. (2017). *Empathetic listening: The Sage encyclopedia of communication research methods*. Accessed at https://methods.sagepub.com/reference/the-sage-encyclopedia-of-communication-research-methods/i4553.xml on December 3, 2019.

Allensworth, E. M., Farrington, C. A., Gordon, M. F., Johnson, D. W., Klein, K., McDaniel, B., et al. (2018). *Supporting social, emotional, & academic development: Research implications for educators*. Chicago: University of Chicago Consortium on School Research. Accessed at https://consortium.uchicago.edu/publications/supporting-social-emotional-academic-development-research-implications-educators on November 23, 2018.

Allington, R. L. (2002). What I've learned about effective reading instruction from a decade of studying exemplary elementary classroom teachers. *Phi Delta Kappan*, *83*(10), 740–747.

American Academy of Pediatrics. (2017). *Children's hospitals admissions for suicidal thoughts, actions double during past decade*. Accessed at www.aappublications.org/news/2017/05/04/PASSuicide050417 on November 8, 2018.

Atwell, N. (2002). *Lessons that change writers*. Portsmouth, NH: Firsthand.

Azzam, A. M. (2014). Motivated to learn: A conversation with Daniel Pink. *Educational Leadership, 72*(1), 12–17. Accessed at www.ascd.org/publications/educational-leadership/sept14/vol72/num01/Motivated-to-Learn@-A-Conversation-with-Daniel-Pink.aspx on October 4, 2019.

Bandura, A. (1977). *Social learning theory.* Englewood Cliffs, NJ: Prentice Hall.

Banfield, S. R., Richmond, V. P., & McCroskey, J. C. (2006). The effect of teacher misbehaviors on teacher credibility and affect for the teacher. *Communication Education, 55*(1), 63–72.

Beckford, A. (2018, August 6). The skills you need to succeed in 2020. *Forbes.* Accessed at www.forbes.com/sites/ellevate/2018/08/06/the-skills-you-need-to-succeed-in-2020/#61104765288a on March 12, 2019.

Begley, S. (2017, May 4). 9 questions with Elizabeth Strout. *Time.* Accessed at https://time.com/4766617/elizabeth-strout on September 27, 2019.

Bennett, J. (2017, June 24). On campus, failure is on the syllabus. *The New York Times.* Accessed at www.nytimes.com/2017/06/24/fashion/fear-of-failure.html on December 1, 2018.

Blow, C. M. (2014, January 23). Reading is fundamental. *The New York Times.* Accessed at www.nytimes.com/2014/01/23/opinion/blow-reading-books-is-fundamental.html on December 8, 2019.

Boogren, T. H. (2018). *Take time for you: Self-care action plans for educators.* Bloomington, IN: Solution Tree Press.

Bosworth, N. (2017, January 18). *Empower students through independent reading* [Blog post]. Accessed at http://edublog.scholastic.com/post/empower-students-through-independent-reading# on June 2, 2019.

Boundless.com. (n.d.). *Listening and critical thinking.* Accessed at http://oer2go.org/mods/en-boundless/www.boundless.com/communications/textbooks/boundless-communications-textbook/learning-to-listen-and-helping-others-do-the-same-5/understanding-listening-29/listening-and-critical-thinking-133-4210/index.html on July 22, 2019.

Bradstreet, A. (n.d.). *To my dear and loving husband.* Accessed at www.poetryfoundation.org/poems/43706/to-my-dear-and-loving-husband on January 7, 2020.

BrainyQuote. (n.d.). *William Styron quotes.* Accessed at https://brainyquote.com/quotes/william_styron_161596 on September 23, 2019.

Brooks, D. (2019, January 17). Students learn from people they love: Putting relationship quality at the center of education. *The New York Times*. Accessed at www.nytimes.com/2019/01/17/opinion/learning-emotion-education.html on March 12, 2019.

Brown, B. (2010). *The gifts of imperfection: Let go of who you think you're supposed to be and embrace who you are*. Center City, MN: Hazelden.

Brown, B. (2012). *Daring greatly: How the courage to be vulnerable transforms the way we live, love, parent, and lead*. New York: Avery.

Brown, B. (2013, January 14). *Shame v. guilt* [Blog post]. Accessed at https://brenebrown.com/blog/2013/01/14/shame-v-guilt on November 22, 2019.

Brown, B. (2017). *Braving the wilderness: The quest for true belonging and the courage to stand alone*. New York: Random House.

Brown, B. (2018, June 7). *Everyone has a story* [Blog post]. Accessed at https://brenebrown.com/blog/2018/06/07/everyone-has-a-story on December 15, 2018.

Burnett, M. (Creator), Spirko, C., Fuchs, K., & Carter, A. (Directors). (2009). *Shark tank* [Television series]. New York: American Broadcasting Company.

CBS Sunday Morning. (2017, November 5). *Ta-Nehisi Coates on the writing process* [Video file]. Accessed at www.youtube.com/watch?v=Z1bOLOmix1Y on January 25, 2019.

Center on the Social and Emotional Foundations for Early Learning. (2005). *Expressing warmth and affection to children*. Accessed at http://csefel.vanderbilt.edu/briefs/wwb20.pdf on March 6, 2020.

Centers for Disease Control and Prevention. (n.d.). *Risk and protective factors*. Accessed at www.cdc.gov/violenceprevention/suicide/riskprotectivefactors.html on September 6, 2019.

Chapman University. (2018, October 16). *America's top fears 2018: Chapman University of American fears* [Blog post]. Accessed at https://blogs.chapman.edu/wilkinson/2018/10/16/americas-top-fears-2018 on March 3, 2019.

Cherry, K. (2018). *How social learning theory works*. Accessed at www.verywellmind.com/social-learning-theory-2795074 on December 15, 2018.

Chiaet, J. (2013, October 4). Novel finding: Reading literary fiction improves empathy. *Scientific American*. Accessed at www.scientificamerican.com/article/novel-finding-reading-literary-fiction-improves-empathy on November 29, 2019.

Cline, E. (2011). *Ready player one*. New York: Broadway.

Coates, T-N. (2015). *Between the world and me*. New York: Spiegel & Grau.

Collins, J. J. (2007). *The Collins writing program: Improving student performance through writing and thinking across the curriculum*. West Newbury, MA: Collins Education.

Columbia University School of Professional Studies. (n.d.). *Narrative medicine*. Accessed at http://sps.columbia.edu/narrative-medicine on March 3, 2019.

Crane, S. (1895). *The red badge of courage*. New York: Appleton.

Daggett, W. R. (2015). *Rigor, relevance, and relationships in action: Innovative leadership and best practices for rapid school improvement*. Rexford, NY: International Center for Leadership in Education.

Dahl, R. (1953). Lamb to the slaughter. *Harper's Magazine*. Accessed at https://bit.ly/1Ij7TVK on September 23, 2019.

Darga, M. (2017, November 18). *Hattie's 2017 updated list of factors influencing student achievement* [Blog post]. Accessed at http://apsuperintendent.edublogs.org/2017/11/18/hatties-2017-updated-list-of-factors-influencing-student-achievement on September 16, 2019.

Darling-Hammond, L., Austin, K., Cheung, M., & Martin, D. (n.d.). *Session 9: Thinking about thinking—Metacognition*. Stanford, CA: Stanford University School of Education. Accessed at www.learner.org/courses/learningclassroom/support/09_metacog.pdf on July 22, 2019.

Darling-Hammond, L., & Cook-Harvey, C. M. (2018). *Educating the whole child: Improving school climate to support student success*. Palo Alto, CA: Learning Policy Institute. Accessed at https://learningpolicyinstitute.org/sites/default/files/product-files/Educating_Whole_Child_REPORT.pdf on March 12, 2019.

Deci, E. L., & Ryan, R. M. (2000). *Self-determination theory (Deci and Ryan)*. Accessed at www.learning-theories.com/self-determination-theory-deci-and-ryan.html on November 23, 2018.

Dewey, J. (1933). *How we think*. Boston: Heath.

Dewey, J. (1938). *Experience and education*. New York: Macmillan.

DiCamillo, K. (2000). *Because of Winn-Dixie*. Somerville, MA: Candlewick Press.

Didion, J. (1976, December 5). Why I write. *The New York Times*. Accessed at www.nytimes.com/1976/12/05/archives/why-i-write-why-i-write.html on September 17, 2019.

Dweck, C. S. (2006). *Mindset: The new psychology of success*. New York: Ballantine Books.

Dweck, C. S. (2015, September 23). Carol Dweck revisits the "growth mindset." *Education Week*. Accessed at www.edweek.org/ew/articles/2015/09/23/carol-dweck-revisits-the-growth-mindset.html on December 1, 2018.

Fadel, C., Trilling, B., & Bialik, M. (2016, August 10). The role of metacognition in learning and achievement. *MindShift*. Accessed at www.kqed.org/mindshift/46038/the-role-of-metacognition-in-learning-and-achievement on December 15, 2018.

Ferlazzo, L. (2018, September 9). *Author interview with Shanna Peeples: "Think like Socrates"* [Blog post]. Accessed at https://blogs.edweek.org/teachers/classroom_qa_with_larry_ferlazzo/2018/09/author_interview_with_shanna_peeples_think_like_socrates.html on March 3, 2019.

Fisher, D. (2016, February 15). *Questioning that deepens comprehension* [Blog post]. Accessed at www.edutopia.org/blog/questioning-that-deepens-comprehension-douglas-fisher-nancy-frey on February 9, 2019.

Fisher, D., & Frey, N. (2014). *Better learning through structured teaching: A framework for the gradual release of responsibility* (2nd ed.). Alexandria, VA: Association for Supervision and Curriculum Development.

Fisher, D., & Frey, N. (2018). Boosting your teacher credibility. *Educational Leadership*, *76*(1), 82–83. Accessed at www.ascd.org/publications/educational-leadership/sept18/vol76/num01/Boosting-Your-Teacher-Credibility.aspx on July 22, 2019.

Flaim, R. F., & Reynolds, E. W., Jr. (Eds.). (1983). *The Holocaust and genocide: A search for conscience*. New York: Anti-Defamation League of B'nai B'rith.

Flavell, J. H. (1979). Metacognition and cognitive monitoring: A new area of cognitive-development inquiry. *American Psychologist*, *34*(10), 906–911.

For the Teachers. (2012). *100 questions for the beginning of school*. Accessed at www.fortheteachers.org/100-questions-for-the-beginning-of-school on January 2, 2019.

Frankl, V. E. (2007). *Man's search for meaning* (60th anniversary ed.). New York: Pocket Books. (Original work published 1959)

Franklin, B. (n.d.). *Project for moral perfection*. Accessed at https://whatsoproudlywehail.org/curriculum/the-meaning-of-america/project-for-moral-perfection on September 25, 2019. (Original work published 1791)

Franklin, B. (1730). *A witch trial at Mount Holly, 22 October 1730*. Accessed at https://founders.archives.gov/documents/Franklin/01-01-02-0056 on January 7, 2020.

Franklin, B. (1922). *The autobiography of Benjamin Franklin*. (F. W. Pine, Ed.). New York: Henry Holt and Company. (Original work published 1793)

Franklin, B. (1849). *Poor Richard's almanac for 1850, as written by Benjamin Franklin for the years 1733–1734–1735*. (J. Doggart, Ed.). New York: Doggart.

Freeman, D. T., & Taylor, G. (n.d.). *Why Shakespeare loved iambic pentameter* [Video file]. Accessed at https://ed.ted.com/lessons/why-shakespeare-loved-iambic-pentameter-david-t-freeman-and-gregory-taylor on December 3, 2019.

Freeman, T., Anderman, L., & Jensen, J. (2007). Sense of belonging in college freshman at the classroom and campus levels. *Journal of Experimental Education*, *75*(3), 203–220.

Friedlaender, D., Burns, D., Lewis-Charp, H., Cook-Harvey, C. M., & Darling-Hammond, L. (2014). *Student-centered schools: Closing the opportunity gap*. Stanford, CA: Stanford Center for Opportunity Policy in Education. Accessed at https://edpolicy.stanford.edu/sites/default/files/scope-pub-student-centered-research-brief.pdf on January 5, 2019.

Frost, R. (n.d.). "The road not taken" [Poem]. Accessed at www.poetryfoundation.org/poems/44272/the-road-not-taken on December 15, 2018. (Original work published 1915)

Gabriel, S., Valenti, J., Naragon-Gainey, K., & Young, A. F. (2017). The psychological importance of collective assembly: Development and validation of the Tendency for Effervescent Assembly Measure (TEAM). *Psychological Assessment*, *29*(11), 1349–1362.

Gallagher, K. (2009). *Readicide: How schools are killing reading and what you can do about it*. Portland, ME: Stenhouse.

Gilbert, E. (2006). *Eat, pray, love: One woman's search for everything across Italy, India and Indonesia*. New York: Viking Press.

Gladwell, M. (2008, December 15). Most likely to succeed: How do we hire when we can't tell who's right for the job? *The New Yorker*. Accessed at www.newyorker.com/magazine/2008/12/15/most-likely-to-succeed-malcolm-gladwell on March 12, 2019.

Goodreads. (n.d.a). *Charles William Eliot quotable quote*. Accessed at https://goodreads.com/quotes/769-books-are-the-quietest-and-most-constant-of-friends-they on September 26, 2019.

Goodreads. (n.d.b). *Christopher Paolini quotable quote*. Accessed at www.goodreads.com/quotes/324186-books-are-my-friends-my-companions-they-make-me-laugh on September 26, 2019.

Goodreads. (n.d.c). *James Baldwin quotable quote*. Accessed at www.goodreads.com/quotes/5853-you-think-your-pain-and-your-heartbreak-are-unprecedented-in on February 9, 2019.

Graff, G. (2003). *Clueless in academe: How schooling obscures the life of the mind*. New Haven, CT: Yale University Press.

Graff, G., & Birkenstein, C. (2010). *"They say / I say:" The moves that matter in academic writing* (2nd ed.). New York: Norton.

Graves, M. F., & Fitzgerald, J. (2003). Scaffolding reading experiences for multilingual classrooms. In G. G. Garcia (Ed.), *English learners: Reaching the highest level of English literacy* (pp. 96–104). Newark, DE: International Reading Association.

Griss, S. (2013, March 20). The power of movement in teaching and learning. *Education Week Teacher*. Accessed at www.edweek.org/tm/articles/2013/03/19/fp_griss.html on November 23, 2019.

Hahn, R. A., & Truman, B. I. (2015). Education improves public health and promotes health equity. *International Journal of Health Services*, *45*(4),657–678.

Haq, H. (2014, March 17). New data says less than 3 percent of children's books surveyed in 2013 were about black people. *Christian Science Monitor*. Accessed at www.csmonitor.com/Books/chapter-and-verse/2014/0317/New-data-says-less-than-3-percent-of-children-s-books-surveyed-in-2013-were-about-black-people on September 17, 2019.

Hattie, J. (2012). *Visible learning for teachers: Maximizing impact on learning*. London: Routledge.

Hawton, K., Saunders, K. E. A., & O'Connor, R. C. (2012). Self-harm and suicide in adolescents. *Lancet*, *379*(9823), 2373–2382.

Headlee, C. (2015, May). *Celeste Headlee: 10 ways to have a better conversation* [Video file]. Accessed at https://ted.com/talks/celeste_headlee_10_ways_to_have_a_better_conversation on March 3, 2019.

Hernández, M. M., Valiente, C., Eisenberg, N., Berger, R. H., Spinrad, T. L., VanSchyndel, S. K., et al. (2017). Elementary students' effortful control and academic achievement: The mediating role of teacher-student relationship quality. *Early Childhood Research Quarterly, 40,* 98–109.

Hinton, S. E. (1967). *The outsiders.* New York: Viking Press.

Homer. (1999). *The odyssey.* London: Penguin. (Original work published 8th century BC)

Hong, K. (2017). *What do I write about? — Editorial brainstorming sheet.* Accessed at https://static01.nyt.com/images/blogs/learning/pdf/2017/KabbyHongBrainstormingSheet.pdf on October 14, 2019.

Hughes, L. (2001). *The collected works of Langston Hughes.* Columbia: University of Missouri Press.

Johnson, D., Johnson, R., & Holubee, E. (2002). *Circles of learning* (5th ed.). Edina, MN: Interaction Books.

Killian, S. (2019). *23 highlights from Hattie 2017.* Accessed at https://evidencebasedteaching.org.au/hatties-2017-updated-list on September 16, 2019.

Kittle, P. (2013). *Book love: Developing depth, stamina, and passion in adolescent readers.* Portsmouth, NH: Heinemann.

Korb, S. (2018, April 21). The soul-crushing student essay. *The New York Times.* Accessed at www.nytimes.com/2018/04/21/opinion/the-soul-crushing-student-essay.html?module=inline on January 25, 2019.

Krashen, S. D. (2004). *The power of reading: Insights from the research* (2nd ed.). Portsmouth, NH: Heinemann.

Labaree, D. (2018). *The five-paragraph fetish.* Accessed at https://aeon.co/essays/writing-essays-by-formula-teaches-students-how-to-not-think on January 25, 2019.

Lamott, A. (1994). *Bird by bird: Some instructions on writing and life.* New York: Pantheon Books.

Lamott, A. (2017a). *13 writing tips, from beloved teacher Anne Lamott.* Accessed at https://ideas.ted.com/14-writing-tips-from-beloved-teacher-anne-lamott on January 25, 2019.

Lamott, A. (2017b). *Hallelujah anyway: Rediscovering mercy.* New York: Riverhead Books.

Lamott, A. (2018a). *Almost everything: Notes on hope.* New York: Riverhead Books.

Lamott, A. (2018b, October). "Show up with hope": Anne Lamott's plan for facing adversity. *National Geographic*. Accessed at www.nationalgeographic.com/magazine/2018/10/embark-essay-anne-lamott-hope-adversity-conflict-climate-change on March 12, 2019.

Lee, H. (1960). *To kill a mockingbird*. Philadelphia: Lippincott.

Lewis, K. (2016, March 10). *Building students' sense of social belonging as a critical first step* [Blog post]. Accessed at https://educationnorthwest.org/northwest-matters/building-students-sense-social-belonging-critical-first-step on December 15, 2018.

Longobardi, C., Prino, L. E., Marengo, D., & Settanni, M. (2016). Student-teacher relationships as a protective factor for school adjustment during the transition from middle to high school. *Frontiers in Psychology*, *7*, 1988.

Lotan, R. A. (2003). Group-worthy tasks. *Educational Leadership*, *60*(6), 72–75.

Lyon, G. E. (1999). *Where I'm from: Where poems come from*. Spring, TX: Absey.

Marzano Resources. (n.d.). *Tips from Dr. Marzano: The highly engaged classroom*. Accessed at https://marzanoresearch.com/resources/tips/hec_tips_archive#tip24 on July 22, 2019.

Maslow, A. H. (1943). A theory of human motivation. *Psychological Review*, *50*(4), 370–396.

Maxwell, J. C. (2007). *Failing forward: Turning mistakes into stepping stones for success*. New York: Nelson.

May, C. (2014). *A learning secret: Don't take notes with a laptop*. Accessed at www.scientificamerican.com/article/a-learning-secret-don-t-take-notes-with-a-laptop on December 1, 2019.

McCombs, B. L. (1995). Understanding the keys to motivation to learn. In *What's noteworthy on learners learning schooling* (pp. 5–12). Aurora, CO: Mid-continent Regional Educational Laboratory.

McKibben, S. (2018). Grit and the greater good: A conversation with Angela Duckworth. *Educational Leadership*, *76*(2), 40–45. Accessed at www.ascd.org/publications/educational-leadership/oct18/vol76/num02/Grit-and-the-Greater-Good@-A-Conversation-with-Angela-Duckworth.aspx on January 25, 2019.

McTighe, J. (2015, August 31). *Three lessons for teachers from Grant Wiggins* [Blog post]. Accessed at http://inservice.ascd.org/three-lessons-for-teachers-from-grant-wiggins on November 23, 2018.

McTighe, J. (2016, March 3). *How should we teach toward success with performance tasks? (Part 7)* [Blog post]. Accessed at https://blog.performancetask.com/how-should-we-teach-toward-success-with-performance-tasks-part-7-93f2279b625 on December 15, 2018.

McTighe, J., & Wiggins, G. (2012). *Understanding by Design framework* [White paper]. Alexandria, VA: Association for Supervision and Curriculum Development. Accessed at www.ascd.org/ASCD/pdf/siteASCD/publications/UbD_WhitePaper0312.pdf on January 25, 2019.

McTighe, J., & Wiggins, G. (2013). *Essential questions: Opening doors to student understanding*. Alexandria, VA: Association for Supervision and Curriculum Development.

McTighe, J., & Willis, J. (2019). *Upgrade your teaching: Understanding by Design meets neuroscience*. Alexandria, VA: Association for Supervision and Curriculum Development.

Mehta, J. (2018, January 4). *A pernicious myth: Basics before deeper learning* [Blog post]. Accessed at http://blogs.edweek.org/edweek/learning_deeply/2018/01/a_pernicious_myth_basics_before_deeper_learning.html on January 25, 2019.

Mehta, J., & Fine, S. (2019, April 26). How to make high schools better for students. *Los Angeles Times*. Accessed at www.latimes.com/opinion/op-ed/la-oe-mehta-fine-education-high-school-excellence-20190426-story.html on November 25, 2019.

Miller, A. (1976). *The crucible*. Lodi, NJ: Everbind Anthologies. (Original work published 1953)

Miller, D. (2009). *The book whisperer: Awakening the reader in every child*. San Francisco: Jossey-Bass.

Mind Matters. (n.d.). *Module 1.4: Relationships and belonging*. Accessed at https://docplayer.net/37678306-Module-1-4-relationships-and-belonging.html on September 14, 2019.

Morrison, T. (1970). *The bluest eye*. New York: Random House.

The Moth. (2016). *Curriculum resources v.1*. New York: Author.

Myers, W. D. (2014, March 16). Where are the people of color in children's books? *The New York Times*. Accessed at https://nytimes.com/2014/03/16/opinion/sunday/where-are-the-people-of-color-in-childrens-books.html on February 9, 2019.

National Commission on Writing in America's Schools and Colleges. (2003). *The neglected "R:" The need for a writing revolution.* Washington, DC: Author. Accessed at www.vantagelearning.com/docs/myaccess/neglectedr.pdf on January 25, 2019.

National Endowment for the Arts. (2007). *To read or not to read: A question of national consequence* (Research Report No. 47). Washington, DC: Author. Accessed at www.arts.gov/sites/default/files/ToRead.pdf on February 9, 2019.

National Institute of Mental Health. (n.d.). *Major depression.* Accessed at www.nimh.nih.gov/health/statistics/major-depression.shtml#part_155031 on November 8, 2018.

Nelson, M. (2018). *Generous listening* [Poem]. Accessed at https://onbeing.org/poetry/generous-listening on December 9, 2018.

Northwest Association for Biomedical Research. (n.d.). *Socratic seminar.* Accessed at www.nwabr.org/sites/default/files/SocSem.pdf on January 7, 2020.

November, A. (2017). *Crafting a vision for empowered learning and teaching: Beyond the $1,000 pencil.* Accessed at https://novemberlearning.com/educational-resources-for-educators/teaching-and-learning-articles/crafting-vision-empowered-learning-teaching-beyond-1000-pencil on February 9, 2019.

Nye, N. S. (n.d.). "Famous" [Poem]. Accessed at www.poetryfoundation.org/poems/47993/famous on May 23, 2019.

Ohlin, B. (2019, November 20). *Active listening: The art of empathetic conversation* [Blog post]. Accessed at https://positivepsychology.com/active-listening on September 19, 2019.

Oliver, M. (2012). "I happened to be standing" [Poem]. In *A thousand mornings: Poems* (pp. 3–4). New York: Penguin Books. Accessed at https://onbeing.org/blog/mary-oliver-reads-her-poem-i-happened-to-be-standing on December 9, 2018.

Oliver, M. (2016). *Upstream: Select essays.* New York: Penguin Press.

Paine, T. (2003). *Common sense and other writings.* (G. S. Wood, Ed.). New York: Modern Library. (Original work published 1776)

Pandolpho, B. (2018a, March 7). Listening is a teacher's most powerful tool. *Education Week Teacher.* Accessed at https://edweek.org/tm/articles/2018/03/07/listening-is-a-teachers-most-powerful-tool.html on August 19, 2019.

Pandolpho, B. (2018b, July 12). Strategies to help your students feel heard. *Edutopia*. Accessed at https://edutopia.org/article/strategies-help-your-students-feel-heard on August 14, 2019.

Pandolpho, B. (2018c, May 4). Putting students in charge of their learning. *Edutopia*. Accessed at www.edutopia.org/article/putting-students-charge-their-learning on November 25, 2019.

Pandolpho, B. (2019, February 20). Reader idea: Helping students discover and write about the issues that matter to them. *The New York Times*. Accessed at www.nytimes.com/2019/02/20/learning/reader-idea-helping-students-discover-and-write-about-the-issues-that-matter-to-them.html on July 23, 2019.

Pandolpho, B., & Wise, M. (2018, November 13). Setting priorities as a new teacher. *Edutopia*. Accessed at https://edutopia.org/article/setting-priorities-new-teacher on August 14, 2019.

Pappas, P. (2010, January 6). *The reflective teacher: A taxonomy of reflection (part 3)* [Blog post]. Accessed at https://peterpappas.com/2010/01/reflective-teacher-taxonomy-reflection.html on December 15, 2018.

Patrick, B. C., Hisley, J., & Kempler, T. (2010). "What's everybody so excited about?" The effects of teacher enthusiasm on student intrinsic motivation and vitality. *Journal of Experimental Education*, *68*(3), 217–236.

Pemberton, S. (Producer, Director). (2014). *Vaccines—Calling the shots* [Motion picture]. Chevy Chase, MD: Tangled Bank Studios.

Perel, E. (2017, October 6). *The quality of our relationships determines the quality of our lives. In Part II of my conversation with Manoush Zomorodi, we talk about keeping our commitments to each other. Who do you owe a phone call to? Who do you need to show up for?* [Facebook update]. Accessed at www.facebook.com/esther.perel/posts/the-quality-of-our-relationships-determines-the-quality-of-our-lives-in-part-ii-/10154911195796711 on July 23, 2019.

Perkins, D. (2009). *Making learning whole: How seven principles of teaching can transform education*. San Francisco: Jossey-Bass.

Pew Research Center. (2017). *U.S. Muslims concerned about their place in society, but continue to believe in the American dream*. Accessed at https://pewforum.org/2017/07/26/findings-from-pew-research-centers-2017-survey-of-us-muslims on July 24, 2019.

Pierson, R. (2013, May). *Rita Pierson: Every kid needs a champion* [Video file]. Accessed at https://ted.com/talks/rita_pierson_every_kid_needs_a_champion?language=en on November 23, 2018.

Pink, D. H. (2009). *Drive: The surprising truth about what motivates us*. New York: Riverhead Books.

Pink, D. H. (2018). *When: The scientific secrets of perfect timing*. New York: Riverhead Books.

Poets.org. (2016). *Haiku: Poetic form*. Accessed at https://poets.org/text/haiku-poetic-form on September 16, 2019.

Purnell, B. (Director). (n.d.). *Why Shakespeare loved iambic pentameter—David T. Freeman and Gregory Taylor* [Video file]. Accessed at https://ed.ted.com/lessons/why-shakespeare-loved-iambic-pentameter-david-t-freeman-and-gregory-taylor on March 3, 2019.

Quindlen, A. (2000). *A short guide to a happy life*. New York: Random House.

Quote Investigator. (n.d.). *That is part of the beauty of all literature. You discover that your longings are universal longings*. Accessed at https://quoteinvestigator.com/2014/03/24/literature/#note-8481- on May 29, 2019.

ReadWriteThink. (n.d.). *Cinquain graphic organizer*. Accessed at www.readwritethink.org/files/resources/lesson_images/lesson43/RWT016-2.pdf on September 16, 2019.

Restrepo, S. (Director). (2019). *Brené Brown: The call to courage* [Documentary film]. United States: Netflix.

Rhodes, J. E. (2018, June 27). *New study shows lifelong influence of mentors: But there's a catch* [Blog post]. Accessed at https://evidencebasedmentoring.org/new-study-shows-lifelong-influence-of-mentors-but-theres-a-catch on September 14, 2019.

Rich, A. (1977). *Claiming an education*. Accessed at www.yorku.ca/cvandaal/files/ClaimingAnEducation.pdf on March 12, 2019.

Riley-Missouri, C. (2018, April 24). *Lots of teachers are super stressed out* [Blog post]. Accessed at https://futurity.org/teachers-stress-1739832 on September 14, 2019.

Robinson, L. R., Leeb, R. T., Merrick, M. T., & Forbes, L. W. (2016). Conceptualizing and measuring safe, stable, nurturing relationships and environments in educational settings. *Journal of Child and Family Studies, 25*(5), 1488–1504. Accessed at www.ncbi.nlm.nih.gov/pmc/articles/PMC5178870 on January 2, 2019.

Rockwell, D. (2018, December 19). *Questions that bring people to life* [Blog post]. Accessed at https://leadershipfreak.blog/2018/12/19/questions-that-bring-people-to-life on February 9, 2019.

Rolland, R. G. (2012). Synthesizing the evidence on classroom goal structures in middle and secondary schools: A meta-analysis and narrative review. *Review of Educational Research, 82*(4), 396–435.

Roosevelt, T. (1910). Citizenship in a republic. *Busy Man's Magazine*. Accessed at https://archive.macleans.ca/article/1910/7/1/citizenship-in-a-republic#!&pid=56 on August 23, 2019.

Roven, C., Nolan, C., Thomas, E., & Snyder, D. (Producers), & Snyder, Z. (Director). (2013). *Man of steel* [Motion picture]. United States: Warner.

Rowell, R. (2013). *Eleanor & Park*. New York: St. Martin's Griffin.

Rowling, J. K. (1997). *Harry Potter and the sorcerer's stone*. New York: Scholastic.

Rush, B. C. (2014, August 28). *Science of storytelling: Why and how to use it in your marketing* [Blog post]. Accessed at https://theguardian.com/media-network/media-network-blog/2014/aug/28/science-storytelling-digital-marketing on March 3, 2019.

Ryan, R. M., & Deci, E. L. (2000). Self-determination theory and the facilitation of intrinsic motivation, social development, and well-being. *American Psychologist, 55*(1), 68–78.

Sadowski, M. (2013). There's always that one teacher. *Educational Leadership, 71*(1), 28–32. Accessed at www.ascd.org/publications/educational-leadership/sept13/vol71/num01/There's-Always-That-One-Teacher.aspx on September 14, 2019.

Schmoker, M. (2006). *Results now: How we can achieve unprecedented improvements in teaching and learning*. Alexandria, VA: Association for Supervision and Curriculum Development.

Shakespeare, W. (1997). Romeo and Juliet. In G. B. Evans & J. J. M. Tobin (Eds.), *The Riverside Shakespeare* (2nd ed., vol. 1, pp. 1055–1100). Boston: Houghton Mifflin. (Original work published 1595)

Simpson, D., & Bruckheimer, J. (Producers), & Smith, J. N. (Director). (1995). *Dangerous minds* [Motion picture]. United States: Buena Vista Pictures.

Smith, E. E. (2017, April). *Emily Esfahani Smith: There's more to life than being happy* [Video file]. Accessed at https://ted.com/talks/emily_esfahani_smith_there_s_more_to_life_than_being_happy on December 15, 2018.

Solomon, A. (2014, March). *Andrew Solomon: How the worst moments in our lives make us who we are* [Video file]. Accessed at https://ted.com/talks/andrew_solomon_how_the_worst_moments_in_our_lives_make_us_who_we_are on March 3, 2019.

Sparks, S. D. (2018, June 19). Getting feedback right: A Q&A with John Hattie. *Education Week*. Accessed at https://edweek.org/ew/articles/2018/06/20/getting-feedback-right-a-qa-with-john.html on March 12, 2019.

Spencer, K. (2015, December 26). New Jersey school district eases pressure on students, baring an ethnic divide. *The New York Times*. Accessed at https://nytimes.com/2015/12/26/nyregion/reforms-to-ease-students-stress-divide-a-new-jersey-school-district.html on November 8, 2018.

St-Amand, J., Girard, S., & Smith, J. (2017). Sense of belonging at school: Defining attributes, determinants, and sustaining strategies. *International Academic Forum Journal of Education*, *5*(2), 105–119. Accessed at https://files.eric.ed.gov/fulltext/EJ1156289.pdf on December 23, 2018.

Stanford Graduate School of Education. (Producer). (2018, July 21). *"Teaching is the profession on which all other professions depend:" Linda Darling-Hammond on transforming education* [Audio podcast]. Accessed at https://ed.stanford.edu/news/teaching-profession-which-all-other-professions-depend-linda-darling-hammond-transforming on January 25, 2019.

State of New Jersey Department of Education. (n.d.). *Standards clarification project: All content areas grades K–12*. Accessed at https://state.nj.us/education/archive/aps/njscp/Phase1allAreas.pdf#page=3 on February 9, 2019.

Steen, M. (2017a, June 26). *Two-way teaching: Embracing the value of students' perspectives* [Blog post]. Accessed at https://education.cu-portland.edu/blog/classroom-resources/embracing-student-voices on May 21, 2019.

Steen, M. (2017b, May 8). *When teachers become better listeners, students become better learners—Here's why* [Blog post]. Accessed at https://education.cu-portland .edu/blog/classroom-resources/teachers-listening-skills on September 18, 2019.

Straehle, C. (2014). Ethical reflections on who is at risk: Vulnerability and global public health. In G. W. Brown, G. Yamey, & S. Wamala (Eds.), *The handbook of global health policy* (pp. 195–207). London: Wiley-Blackwell.

Strunk, W., Jr., & White, E. B. (1959). *The elements of style*. New York: Macmillan.

Sulla, N. (2019). *Students taking charge in grades K–5: Inside the learner-active, technology-infused classroom* (2nd ed.). New York: Routledge.

Sztabnik, B. (n.d.). *TWT #2—Grant Wiggins* [Audio podcast]. Accessed at http://talkswithteachers.com/twt-2-grant-wiggins on January 5, 2019.

Taylor, E. (n.d.). "Huswifery" [Poem]. Accessed at https://poetryfoundation.org/poems/46133/huswifery on September 25, 2019.

Tippett, K. (Producer). (2018a, September 13). *Eula Biss: Let's talk about whiteness* [Audio podcast]. Accessed at https://onbeing.org/programs/eula-biss-lets-talk-about-whiteness-sep2018 on March 3, 2019.

Tippett, K. (Producer). (2018b, September 27). *Frances Kissling: What is good in the position of the other* [Audio podcast]. Accessed at https://onbeing.org/programs/frances-kissling-what-is-good-in-the-position-of-the-other-sep2018 on March 3, 2019.

Tippett, K. (Producer). (2018c, July 12). *Luis Alberto Urrea: What borders are really about, and what we do with them* [Audio podcast]. Accessed at https://onbeing.org/programs/luis-alberto-urrea-what-borders-are-really-about-and-what-we-do-with-them-jul2018 on July 23, 2019.

Tippett, K. (Producer). (2018d, March 15). *Naomi Shihab Nye: Your life is a poem* [Audio podcast]. Accessed at https://onbeing.org/programs/naomi-shihab-nye-your-life-is-a-poem-mar2018 on January 25, 2019.

Tippett, K. (Producer). (2018e, September 6). *Pádraig Ó Tuama and Marilyn Nelson: Choosing words that deepen the argument of being alive* [Audio podcast]. Accessed at https://onbeing.org/programs/padraig-o-tuama-marilyn-nelson-choosing-words-that-deepen-the-argument-of-being-alive-sep2018 on December 15, 2018.

Tippett, K. (Producer). (2019a, January 10). *Claudia Rankine: How can I say this so we can stay in this car together?* [Audio podcast]. Accessed at https://onbeing.org/programs/claudia-rankine-how-can-i-say-this-so-we-can-stay-in-this-car-together-jan2019 on November 24, 2019.

Tippett, K. (Producer). (2019b, February 7). *Maria Popova: Cartographer of meaning in a digital age* [Audio podcast]. Accessed at https://onbeing.org/programs/maria-popova-cartographer-of-meaning-in-a-digital-age-feb2019/#transcript on March 3, 2019.

Tippett, K. (Producer). (2019c, February 14). *Richard Davidson: A neuroscientist on love and learning* [Audio podcast]. Accessed at https://onbeing.org/programs/richard-davidson-a-neuroscientist-on-love-and-learning-feb2019 on March 12, 2019.

Treasure, J. (2013, June). *Julian Treasure: How to speak so that people want to listen* [Video file]. Accessed at www.ted.com/talks/julian_treasure_how_to_speak_so_that_people_want_to_listen?language=en on December 3, 2019.

Twardosz, S. (2005). *Expressing warmth and affection to children*. Accessed at http://csefel.vanderbilt.edu/briefs/wwb20.pdf on November 23, 2019.

United States Holocaust Memorial Museum. (n.d.). *Teaching about the Holocaust: Assessing and defining responsibility*. Accessed at www.ushmm.org/m/pdfs/20121130-resp-ex-worksheet.pdf on September 14, 2019.

University of Minnesota. (n.d.). *The ABC of it: Why children's books matter.* Accessed at www.lib.umn.edu/clrc/kerlan-collection on January 25, 2019.

University of Oxford. (2011, May 9). Reading at 16 linked to better job prospects. *ScienceDaily*. Accessed at www.sciencedaily.com/releases/2011/05/110504150539.htm on February 9, 2019.

Wakefield, A. J., Murch, S. H., Anthony, A., Linnell, J., Casson, D. M., Malik, M., et al. (1998). Ileal-lymphoid-nodular hyperplasia, non-specific colitis, and pervasive developmental disorder in children. *Lancet, 351*(9103), 637–641.

Warner, J. (2018). *Why they can't write: Killing the five-paragraph essay and other necessities*. Baltimore: Johns Hopkins University Press.

Weinstein, A. (2016, February 24). Don't turn away from the art of life. *The New York Times*. Accessed at https://nytimes.com/2016/02/24/opinion/dont-turn-away-from-the-art-of-life.html on September 17, 2019.

West, J. (1957). *To see the dream*. San Diego: Harcourt, Brace.

Whitman, W. (1881). *Leaves of grass*. London: Bogue.

Wiesel, E. (2006). *Night* (M. Wiesel, Trans.). London: Hill & Wang. (Original work published 1960)

Wiggins, A. (2017). *The best class you never taught: How spider web discussion can turn students into learning leaders*. Alexandria, VA: Association for Supervision and Curriculum Development.

Wiggins, G. (2010, March 27). *What is transfer?* [Blog post]. Accessed at www.authenticeducation.org/ae_bigideas/article.lasso?artid=60 on November 23, 2018.

Wiggins, G. (2012). Seven keys to effective feedback. *Educational Leadership, 70*(1), 10–16. Accessed at www.ascd.org/publications/educational-leadership/sept12/vol70/num01/Seven-Keys-to-Effective-Feedback.aspx on December 15, 2018.

Wiggins, G. (2013, September 9). *Beyond teacher egocentrism: Design thinking* [Blog post]. Accessed at https://grantwiggins.wordpress.com/2013/09/09/beyond-teacher-egocentrism-design-thinking on November 23, 2018.

Wiggins, G. (2014, April 19). *Engagement and personalization: Feedback part 2* [Blog post]. Accessed at https://grantwiggins.wordpress.com/2014/04/19/engagement-and-personalization-feedback-part-2 on March 12, 2019.

Wiggins, G. (2015, March 26). *On reading, part 4: Research on the comprehension strategies—A closer look* [Blog post]. Accessed at https://grantwiggins.wordpress.com/2015/03/26/on-reading-part-4-research-on-the-comprehension-strategies-a-closer-look on February 9, 2019.

Wiggins, G., & McTighe, J. (2005). *Understanding by Design* (Expanded 2nd ed.). Alexandria, VA: Association for Supervision and Curriculum Development.

Wiggins, G., & McTighe, J. (2008). Put understanding first. *Educational Leadership, 65*(8), 36–41. Accessed at www.ascd.org/publications/educational-leadership/may08/vol65/num08/Put-Understanding-First.aspx on August 23, 2019.

Wiggins, G., & McTighe, J. (2012). *The Understanding by Design guide to advanced concepts in creating and reviewing units.* Alexandria, VA: Association for Supervision and Curriculum Development.

Wiliam, D. (2013). Assessment: The bridge between teaching and learning. *Voices from the Middle, 21*(2), 15–20.

Willems, M. (2007). *Today I will fly!* New York: Scholastic.

Winfrey, O. (2017). *The wisdom of Sundays: Life-changing insights from Super Soul conversations.* New York: Flatiron Books.

Wormeli, R. (2011). Redos and retakes done right. *Educational Leadership, 69*(3), 22–26.

Wormeli, R. (2016). What to do in week one? *Educational Leadership, 74*(1), 10–15. Accessed at ww.ascd.org/publications/educational-leadership/sept16/vol74/num01/What-to-Do-in-Week-One%C2%A2.aspx on March 6, 2020.

Wormeli, R. (2018a, April 9). Fair isn't always equal—3 grading malpractices. *MiddleWeb*. Accessed at www.middleweb.com/37435/fair-isnt-always-equal-3-grading-malpractices on December 15, 2018.

Wormeli, R. (2018b, April). The grief of accepting new ideas. *AMLE Magazine*. Accessed at www.amle.org/BrowsebyTopic/WhatsNew/WNDet/TabId/270/ArtMID/888/ArticleID/911/The-Grief-of-Accepting-New-Ideas.aspx on March 12, 2019.

Wu, T. (2018, February 16). The tyranny of convenience. *The New York Times*. Accessed at www.nytimes.com/2018/02/16/opinion/sunday/tyranny-convenience.html on January 5, 2019.

Zak, P. J. (2014, October 28). *Why your brain loves good storytelling*. Accessed at https://hbr.org/2014/10/why-your-brain-loves-good-storytelling on December 4, 2019.

Zucker, L. (2016). Under discussion: Teaching speaking and listening. *English Journal, 105*(5), 92–94. Accessed at www.northernhighlands.org/cms/lib/NJ01000179/Centricity/Domain/50/Zucker2016ReadingCloselyDiscussingMeaningfully.pdf on September 20, 2019.

Index

D

H

I

K

L

M

S

Y

Z

Every Teacher Is a Literacy Teacher Series
Edited by Mark Onuscheck and Jeanne Spiller
Written by acclaimed experts and practitioners, the *Every Teacher Is a Literacy Teacher* series details how to promote literacy growth across disciplines and grade bands. Learn how to build a common language, work in collaborative teams, implement literacy-infused instruction, and more.
BKF904, BKF907, BKF901, BKF915, BKF902

Loving What They Learn
Alexander McNeece
Deep learning and high engagement are possible for all students, regardless of subject, grade, or previous experience. With *Loving What They Learn*, you will discover how to quantifiably measure students' needs, help strengthen their academic self-concept, and increase their self-efficacy.
BKF917

The New Art and Science of Teaching Reading
Julia A. Simms and Robert J. Marzano
The New Art and Science of Teaching Reading presents a compelling model for reading development structured around five key topic areas. More than 100 reading-focused instructional strategies are laid out in detail to help teachers ensure every student becomes a proficient reader.
BKF811

The New Art and Science of Teaching Writing
Kathy Tuchman Glass and Robert J. Marzano
Using a clear and well-organized structure, the authors apply the strategies originally laid out in *The New Art and Science of Teaching* to the teaching of writing. In total, the book explores more than 100 strategies for teaching writing across grade levels and subject areas.
BKF796

Solution Tree | Press 

Visit SolutionTree.com or call 800.733.6786 to order.

GLOBAL PD

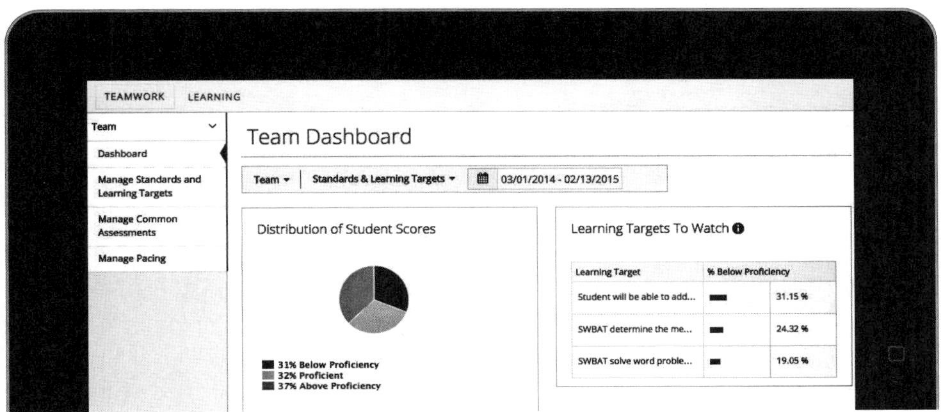

The **Power to Improve** Is in Your Hands

Global PD gives educators focused and goals-oriented training from top experts. You can rely on this innovative online tool to improve instruction in every classroom.

- Get unlimited, on-demand access to guided video and book content from top Solution Tree authors.
- Improve practices with personalized virtual coaching from PLC-certified trainers.
- Customize learning based on skill level and time commitments.